PYTHON PROGRAMMING FOR

BEGINNERS

THE UPDATED GUIDE TO LEARN PYTHON PROGRAMMING STEP BY
STEP WITH PRACTICAL EXAMPLES AND THE BASICS OF MACHINE
LEARNING, MASTER COMPUTER LANGUAGES IN A FEW DAYS
(VOL.1)

AUTHOR

BILL STEVEN

This document is geared towards providing exact and reliable information with regards to the topic and issue covered. The publication is sold with the idea that the publisher is not required to render accounting, officially permitted, or otherwise, qualified services. If advice is necessary, legal or professional, a practiced individual in the profession should be ordered.

- From a Declaration of Principles which was accepted and approved equally by a Committee of the American Bar Association and a Committee of Publishers and Associations.

Table of contents

Contents

PYTHON PROGRAMMING FOR BEGINNERS

THE UPDATED GUIDE TO LEARN PYTHON PROGRAMMING STEP BY STEP WITH PRACTICAL EXAMPLES AND THE BASICS OF MACHINE LEARNING, MASTER COMPUTER LANGUAGES IN A FEW DAYS (VOL.1)

INTRODUCTION

What is Python?

Python is a well-known programming language. It was originated by Guido van Rossum and discharged in 1991. Python is an exceptionally straightforward yet amazing article situated programming language. The syntax of Python is straightforward, so a novice can learn Python easily. Python is created by Guido van Rossum. Guido van Rossum began actualizing Python in 1989. Python is an extremely basic programming language, so regardless of whether you are new to programming, you can learn python without confronting any issues.

Python is named after the satire network shows Monty Python's Flying Circus. It isn't named after the Python snake.

It is utilized for:

- Web improvement (server-side),

- Software improvement,

- Mathematics,

- System scripting.

- Python may be used on a server to make web applications.

- Python can be utilized close by programming to make work processes.

- Python can associate with database frameworks. It can likewise peruse and adjust documents.

- Python can be utilized to deal with enormous information and perform complex arithmetic.

- Python can be utilized for quick prototyping, or for generation prepared programming improvement.

Why Python?

- Python deals with various stages (Windows, Mac, Linux, Raspberry Pi, and so on).

- Python has a straightforward syntax like the English language.

- Python has a syntax that enables designers to compose programs with fewer lines than some other programming language.

- Python runs on a translator framework, implying that code can be executed when it is composed. This implies prototyping can be speedy.

- Python can be treated in a procedural manner, and an article orientated way or a functional way.

Great to know

- The latest significant form of Python will be Python 3, which we will use in this instructional exercise. In any case, Python 2, in spite of the fact that not being refreshed with something besides security refreshes, is still very well known.

- In this instructional ebook exercise, Python will be written in a word processor. It is easy to compose Python in an Integrated Development Environment, for instance, Thonny, Pycharm, Netbeans, or Eclipse, which are especially valuable when overseeing bigger assortments of Python records.

Python Syntax contrasted with other programming language.

- Python was intended for comprehensibility and had a few similitudes to the English language with an impact from science.

- Python uses new lines to finish an order, instead of other programming language which frequently use semicolons or brackets.

- Python depends on indentation, utilizing whitespace, to characterize scope, for example, the extent of circles, functions, and classes. Other programming language frequently utilize wavy sections for this reason.

Highlights of Python programming language

1. Comprehensible: Python is an entirely meaningful language.

2. Simple to Learn: Learning python is simple as this is an expressive and elevated level programming language, which implies it is straightforward the language and, therefore, simple to learn.

3. Cross stage: Python is accessible and can run on different working frameworks, for example, Mac, Windows, Linux, Unix, and so on. This makes it a cross-stage and versatile language.

4. Open Source: Python is an open-source programming language.

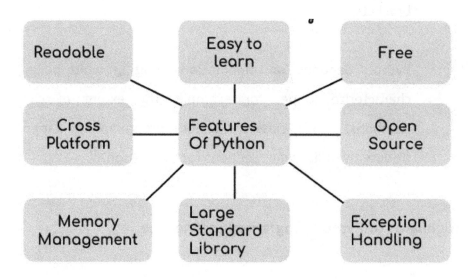

5. Enormous standard library: Python accompanies a huge standard library that has some helpful codes and functions which we can utilize while composing code in Python.

6. Free: Python can be downloaded and used. This indicates that you can download it for nothing and use it in your application. Python has a case of a FLOSS (Free/Libre Open Source Software), which implies you can uninhibitedly circulate duplicates of this product, read its source code, and change it.

7. Supports exemption taking care of: If you are new, you may think about what is a special case? An exemption is an occasion that can happen during special program cases and can disturb the ordinary progression of the program. Python underpins special cases dealing with which implies we can compose less error inclined code and can test different situations that can cause an exemption later on.

8. Propelled highlights: Supports generators and list understandings. We will cover these highlights later.

9. Programmed memory the executives: Python underpins programmed memory the board, which implies the memory is cleared and liberated naturally. You don't need to try clearing the memory.

What Can You Do with Python?

You might be thinking about what all the utilizations of Python are. There are such a large number of utilizations of Python, here is a portion of them.

1. Web advancement – Web systems like Django and Flask depend on Python. They assist you with composing server-side code, which encourages you to oversee database, compose backend programming rationale, mapping URLs, and so forth.

2. AI – There are many AI applications written in Python. AI is an approach to compose a rationale with the goal that a machine can learn and take care of a specific issue alone. For instance, items suggestion in sites like Amazon, Flipkart, eBay, and so forth is an AI calculation that recognizes a client's advantage. Face acknowledgment and Voice acknowledgment in your telephone is another case of AI.

3. Information Analysis – Data examination and information representation in the type of graphs can likewise be created utilizing Python.

4. Scripting – Scripting is composing little projects to mechanize straightforward errands, for example, sending computerized reaction

messages and so forth. Such type of utilizations can likewise be written in Python programming language.

5. Game advancement – You can create games utilizing Python.

6. You can create embedded applications in Python.

7. Work area applications – You can create work area applications in Python utilizing libraries like TKinter or QT.

The most effective method to introduce Python

Python establishment is quite straightforward, and you can introduce it on any working framework, for example, Windows, Mac OS X, Ubuntu, and so on.

PYTHON'S HISTORY

Python was considered in the late 1980s by Guido van Rossum at CWI in the Netherlands as a successor of the ABC programming language equipped for special case taking care of and interfacing with the Amoeba working framework. Van Rossum is Python's chief creator, and his proceeding with the focal job in choosing the course of Python is recognized by alluding to him as its Benevolent Dictator forever (BDFL).

In 1991, van Rossum distributed the code (marked form 0.9.0) to alt.sources. Effectively present at this phase being developed were classes with legacy, special case taking care of, functions, and the center datatypes of the list, dict, str, etc.

Additionally, in this underlying discharge was a module framework obtained from Modula-3; van Rossum portrays the module as "one of Python's significant programming units."

Python's special case model additionally takes after Modula-3's, with the option of an else provision.

In 1994, comp.lang.python, the essential talk discussion for Python, was framed, denoting an achievement in the development of Python's userbase.

Python arrived at form 1.0 in January 1994. A significant arrangement of highlights remembered for this discharge was the functional programming apparatuses lambda, map, filter, and decrease. Van Rossum states that "Python obtained lambda, diminish (), channel () and guide (), the kindness of (I accept) a Lisp programmer who missed them and submitted working patches." The real patron was Amrit Prem; no particular notice of any Lisp legacy is referenced in the discharge notes at the time.

The last form discharged from CWI was Python 1.2. In 1995, van Rossum proceeded with his work on Python at the Corporation for National Research Initiatives (CNRI) in Reston, Virginia, where he discharged a few renditions of the product.

By form 1.4, Python had gained a few new highlights. Prominent among these are the Modula-3 enlivened watchword contentions (which are additionally like Common Lisp's catchphrase contentions), and inherent help for complex numbers. Additionally included is an essential type of information covering up by name ruining; however, this is effectively skirted.

During van Rossum's stay at CNRI, he propelled the Computer Programming for Everybody (CP4E) activity, expecting to make programming progressively open to more individuals, with an essential 'proficiency' in programming language, like the fundamental English education and arithmetic aptitudes required by most businesses. Python served a focal job in this: as a result of its attention on clean syntax, it was at that point appropriate, and CP4E's objectives bore similitudes to its antecedent, ABC. The venture was financed by DARPA. Starting in 2007, the CP4E venture is latent, and keeping in mind that Python endeavors to be effectively learnable and not very arcane in its syntax and semantics, contacting non-software engineers isn't a functioning concern.

In 2000, the Python center improvement group moved to BeOpen.com to shape the BeOpen PythonLabs group. CNRI mentioned that form 1.6 be discharged, condensing Python's advancement up to where the improvement group left CNRI. Subsequently, the discharge plans for 1.6 and 2.0 had a lot of covers. Python 2.0 was the solitary discharge from BeOpen.com. After Python 2.0 was discharged by BeOpen.com, Guido van Rossum and the different PythonLabs designers joined Digital Creations.

Python 2.0 acquired a significant element from the functional programming language Haskell: list appreciations. Python's syntax for this build is fundamentally the same as Haskell's, aside from Haskell's inclination for punctuation characters and Python's inclination for alphabetic watchwords. Python 2.0 additionally presented a trash assortment framework fit for gathering reference cycles.

Following this twofold discharge, and after van Rossum left CNRI to work with business programming designers, it turned out to be evident that the capacity to utilize Python with programming accessible under the GPL was entirely alluring. The permit utilized around then, the Python License, incorporated a condition expressing that the permit was administered by the State of Virginia, which made it, in perspective on the Free Software Foundation's (FSF) legal advisors, contradictory with the GNU GPL. CNRI and the FSF cooperated to create empowering wording changes to Python's free programming permit that would make it GPL-good.

That year (2001), van Rossum was granted the FSF Award for the Advancement of Free Software.

Python 1.6.1 is basically equivalent to Python 1.6, with a couple of minor bug fixes, and with the new GPL-perfect permit.

Python 2.1 was a subordinate work of Python 1.6.1, just as of Python 2.0. Its permit was renamed Python Software Foundation License. All code, documentation, and details included, from the hour of Python 2.1's alpha discharge on, is claimed by the Python Software Foundation (PSF), a non-benefit association framed in 2001, displayed after the Apache Software Foundation. Remembered for this discharge (however off as a matter of course and not compulsory until a few forms later) was usage of checking progressively like static perusing (of which Scheme is the originator) rules.

A significant advancement in Python 2.2 was the unification of Python's (types written in C), and classes (types written in Python) into one chain of importance. This single unification made Python's item model simply and reliably object arranged. Additionally included were generators which were enlivened by Icon.

Python's standard library options and grammatical decisions were firmly affected by Java at times: the logging bundle, presented in adaptation 2.3, the SAX parser, presented in 2.0, and the decorator design syntax that utilizations @, included rendition 2.4

Early history

In February 1991, van Rossum distributed the code (named variant 0.9.0) to alt.sources. This happened 3 years after the introductory arrival of Perl and before the main book on Perl was distributed. Larry Wall started to deal with Perl in 1987, while filling in as a software engineer at Unisys and discharged variant 1.0 to the comp.sources. Misc newsgroup on December 18, 1987. In 1991, Programming Perl, referred to numerous Perl developers as the "Camel Book" due to its spread, was distributed and turned into the true reference for the language.

Effectively present at this phase being developed were classes with legacy, special case taking care of, functions, and the center datatypes of a list, dict, str, etc. Likewise, in this underlying discharge was a module framework obtained from Modula-3; Van Rossum portrays the module as "one of Python's significant programming units." Python's exemption model additionally looks like Modula-3's, with the option of an else proviso.

In 1994 comp.lang. Python, the essential talk gathering for Python, was shaped, denoting an achievement in the development of Python's userbase.

VERSION 1

Python arrived at form 1.0 in January 1994. Perl 5.000 was discharged on October 17, 1994.

The major new highlights remembered for this discharge were the functional programming devices lambda, guide, channel, and lessen.

Van Rossum expressed that "Python obtained lambda, lessen(), channel() and guide(), civility of a Lisp programmer who missed them and submitted working patches."

The last form discharged while Van Rossum was at CWI was Python 1.2. In 1995, Van Rossum proceeded with his work on Python at the Corporation for National Research Initiatives (CNRI) in Reston, Virginia, whence he discharged a few variants.

By adaptation 1.4, Python had procured a few new highlights. Prominent among these are the Modula-3 motivated watchword contentions (which are likewise comparable to common Lisp's catchphrase contentions) and implicit help for complex numbers. Additionally included is an essential type of information stowing away by name disfiguring. However, this is effectively avoided.

During Van Rossum's stay at CNRI, he propelled the Computer Programming for Everybody (CP4E) activity, expecting to make programming progressively open to more individuals, with a fundamental "proficiency" in programming language, like the essential English education and science aptitudes required by most businesses. Python served a focal job in this: on account of its emphasis on clean syntax, it was at that point appropriate, and CP4E's objectives bore likenesses to its forerunner, ABC. The task was financed by DARPA. Starting in 2007, the CP4E venture is latent and keeping in mind that Python endeavors to be effectively learnable and not very arcane in its syntax and semantics, connecting with non-software engineers isn't a functioning concern.

Variant 2 and BeOpen

Perl 5.6 was discharged on March 22, 2000. In 2000, the Python center improvement group moved to BeOpen.com to shape the BeOpen PythonLabs group. CNRI mentioned that a rendition 1.6 be discharged, abridging Python's improvement up to where the advancement group left CNRI. Thusly, the discharge plans for 1.6 and 2.0 had a lot of covers. Python 2.0 likewise presented a trash assortment framework fit for gathering reference cycles.

Python 2.0 was the main discharge from BeOpen.com. After Python 2.0 was discharged by BeOpen.com, Guido van Rossum and the different PythonLabs engineers joined Digital Creations.

The Python 1.6 discharge incorporated another CNRI permit that was significantly longer than the CWI permit that had been utilized for before discharges. The new permit incorporated a provision expressing that the permit was represented by the laws of the State of Virginia. The Free Software Foundation contended that the decision of-law statement was inconsistent with the GNU General Public License. BeOpen, CNRI, and the FSF arranged a change to Python's free programming permit that would make it GPL-perfect. Python 1.6.1 is basically equivalent to Python 1.6, with a couple of minor bug fixes, and with the new GPL-perfect permit.

Python 2.0 presented list cognizances, an element obtained from the functional programming language SETL and Haskell. Python's syntax for this build is fundamentally the same as Haskell's, aside from Haskell's inclination for punctuation characters and Python's inclination for alphabetic catchphrases.

Python 2.1 was near Python 1.6.1, just as Python 2.0. Its permit was renamed Python Software Foundation License. All code, documentation, and details included, from the hour of Python 2.1's alpha discharge on, is possessed by the Python Software Foundation (PSF), a non-benefit association framed in 2001, demonstrated after the Apache Software Foundation. The discharge incorporated a change to the language detail to help settled extensions as other statically perused language. (The component was killed as a matter of course, and not required, until Python 2.2.)

A significant development in Python 2.2 was the unification of Python's (types written in C) and classes (types written in Python) into one chain of importance. This single unification made Python's item model simply and reliably object situated. Additionally included were generators which were enlivened by Icon.

Python 2.6 was discharged to match with Python 3.0, and incorporated a few highlights from that discharge, just as an "admonitions" mode that featured the utilization of highlights that were evacuated in Python 3.0. Thus, Python 2.7 matched with and included highlights from Python 3.1, which was discharged on June 26, 2009. Parallel 2.x and 3.x discharges at that point stopped, and Python 2.7 was the last discharge in the 2.x arrangement.

In November 2014, it was reported that Python 2.7 would be upheld until 2020, yet clients were urged to move to Python 3 at the earliest opportunity.

Version 3

Python 3.0 (likewise called "Python 3000" or "Py3K") was discharged on December 3, 2008. It was intended to amend central plan defects in the language—the progressions required couldn't be actualized while holding full in reverse similarity with the 2.x arrangement, which required another significant adaptation number. The core value of Python 3 was: "lessen include duplication by evacuating old methods for getting things done."

Python 3.0 was created in a similar way of thinking, as in earlier forms. Be that as it may, as Python had amassed new and repetitive approaches to program a similar errand, Python 3.0 had an accentuation on expelling duplicative develops and modules, with regards to "There ought to be one—and ideally just one — evident approach to do it."

In any case, Python 3.0 stayed a multi-worldview language. Coders still had choices among object-direction, organized programming, functional programming, and different ideal models, yet inside such expansive decisions, the subtleties were expected to be more evident in Python 3.0 than they were in Python 2.x.

Similarity

Python 3.0 broke in reverse similarity, and much Python 2 code doesn't run unmodified on Python 3. Python's dynamic composing joined with the designs to change the semantics of specific techniques for lexicons, for instance, made ideal mechanical interpretation from Python 2.x to Python 3.0 troublesome.

A device called "2to3" does the pieces of interpretation that should be possible consequently. At this, 2to3 gave off an impression of being genuinely fruitful; however an early audit noticed that there were parts of interpretation that such an apparatus could always be unable to deal with. Before the turn out of Python 3, ventures requiring similarity with both the 2.x and 3.x arrangement were prescribed to have one hotspot (for the 2.x arrangement), and produce discharges for the Python 3.x stage utilizing 2to3. Alters to the Python 3.x code were disheartened for such a long time as the code expected to run on Python 2.x. This is never again prescribed; starting in 2012, the favored option is to make a solitary code base that can run under both Python 2 and 3 utilizing similarity modules.

Highlights

A portion of the significant changes included for Python 3.0 were:

• Changing print with the goal that it is a worked in function, not a statement. This made it simpler to change a module to utilize an alternate print function, just as making the syntax progressively ordinary. In Python 2.6 & 2.7, print() is accessible as a builtin yet is concealed by the print statement syntax, which can be incapacitated by entering from __future__ import print_function at the highest point of the record.

• Removal of the Python 2 information function, and the renaming of the raw_input function to enter. Python 3's information function carries on like Python 2's raw_input function, in that the information is constantly returned as a string as opposed to being assessed as an articulation.

• Moving decrease (yet not guide or sift) out of the implicit namespace and into functools (the method of reasoning being that activities utilizing diminish are communicated all the more plainly utilizing an aggregation circle);

• Adding support for discretionary function explanations that can be utilized for casual type revelations or different purposes;

• Unifying the str/unicode types, speaking to content, and presenting a different changeless bytes type; and a generally comparing alterable bytearraytype, the two of which speak to varieties of bytes;

• Removing in reverse similarity highlights, including old-style classes, string special cases, and understood relative imports.

• A change in number division functionality. (In Python 2, 5/2 will be 2. In Python 3, 5/2 is 2.5, and 5/2 will be 2).

Consequent discharges in the Python 3.x arrangement have incorporated extra, considerable new highlights; all continuous advancement of the language is done in the 3.x arrangement.

Python 3.7.3 is the most recent adaptation.

The two of the most utilized adaptations need to Python 2.x and 3.x. There is a great deal of rivalry between the two, and them two appear to have a lot of various fanbase.

For different purposes, for example, creating, scripting, age, and programming testing, this language is used. Because of its style and straightforwardness, top innovation associations like Dropbox, Google, Quora, Mozilla, Hewlett-Packard, Qualcomm, IBM, and Cisco have executed Python.

Python has made considerable progress in turning into the most famous coding language on the planet. Python has quite recently turned 30, however despite everything it has that obscure appeal and X factor which can be obviously observed from the way that Google clients have reliably looked for Python substantially more than they have scanned for Kim Kardashian, Donald Trump, Tom Cruise and so forth.

Python has been a motivation for some other coding language, for example, Ruby, Cobra, Boo, CoffeeScript ECMAScript, Groovy, Swift Go, OCaml, Julia, and so on.

WHY IS PYTHON THE BEST OF OTHERS

The upsides of python over different languages.

Python is regularly contrasted with other deciphered language, for example, Java, JavaScript, Perl, Tcl, or Smalltalk. Comparism with C++, Common Lisp, and Scheme can likewise be illuminating. In this sense, I will quickly contrast Python with every one of these language. These correlations focus on language gives as it were. For all intents and purposes, the choice of a programming language is as often as possible coordinated by other authentic prerequisites, for instance, cost, openness, planning, and prior endeavor, or even energetic association. Since these edges are significantly factor, it gives off an impression of being a pointless activity to consider them much for this assessment.

Java

Python programming are commonly expected to run slower than Java programs, yet they additionally set aside substantially less effort to create. Python programming are commonly 3-5 times shorter than equal Java programs. This distinction can be prescribed to Python's worked in elevated level information types, and it is dynamic composing. For instance, a Python developer burns through no time proclaiming the types of contentions or factors, and Python's incredible polymorphic list and lexicon types, for which rich syntactic help is incorporated straight with the language, discover a utilization in pretty much every Python program. In light of the run-time composing, Python's running time must work harder than Java's. While assessing the articulation a+b, it should initially review the items a and b to discover their type, which isn't known at the accumulate time. It, at that point, conjures the fitting expansion activity, which might be an over-burden client characterized technique. Java, then again, can play out a whole proficient number or coasting point expansion, yet requires variable announcements for an and b, and doesn't permit over-burdening of the + operator for occurrences of client characterized classes.

Thus, Python is greatly improved fit as a "stick" language, while Java is better described as a low-level usage language. Truth be told, the two together make an amazing mix. Parts can be created in Java and consolidated to shape applications in Python; Python can likewise be utilized to prototype segments until their plan can be "solidified" in a Java usage. To assist this with composing of headway, a Python execution written in Java is being taken a shot at, which grants calling Python code from Java and the a different way. In this use, Python source code is implied Java bytecode (with help from a run-time library to support Python's dynamic semantics).

Javascript

Python's "object-based" subset is commonly proportionate to JavaScript. Like JavaScript (and not in the least like Java), Python supports a programming style that usages clear functions and factors without partaking in class definitions. In any case, for JavaScript, that is everything that issues. Python, on the other hand, supports making much greater tasks and better code reuse through a veritable article orchestrated programming style, where classes and heritage expect a noteworthy activity.

Perl

Python and Perl start from an equivalent establishment (Unix scripting, which both have long outgrown) and sport various tantamount features. In any case, they have an alternate perspective. Perl underscores support for common application-arranged assignments, for instance, by having worked in standard verbalizations, record sifting, and report making features. Python underscores support for common programming frameworks, for instance, data structure plan and article masterminded to program, and urges programming designers to make important (and along these lines reasonable) code by giving a rich yet not exorbitantly puzzling documentation. Subsequently, Python approaches Perl yet only here and there beats it in its one of a kind application space; at any rate, Python has importance well past Perl's forte.

Tcl

Like Python, Tcl is also used as an application expansion language, similarly as an autonomous programming language. In any case, Tcl, which usually stores all data as strings, is fragile on data structures and executes standard code much more slow than Python. Tcl similarly needs requiring for forming enormous undertakings, for instance, estimated namespaces. While an "ordinary" gigantic application using Tcl ordinarily contains Tcl developments written in C or C++ that are express to that application, a proportionate Python application can consistently be written in "unadulterated Python." Obviously, unadulterated Python headway is much speedier than forming and examine a C or C++ portion. Tcl's is one redeeming quality is the Tk tool stash. Python has grasped an interface to Tk as its standard GUI portion library.

Tcl 8.0 watches out for the speed issues by giving a bytecode compiler limited data type backing and incorporates namespaces. It is up 'til now an altogether progressively cumbersome programming language.

C++

Almost everything said for Java in like manner applies for C++, essentially more so: where Python code is commonly 3-5 times shorter than similar Java code, it is oftentimes 5-10 times shorter than corresponding C++ code! Account confirmation suggests that one Python programming specialist can finish in two months what two C++ designers can't complete in a year.

Meanwhile, Python shines as a glue language used to unite portions written in C++.

The Python people group's attention on giving amicable acquaintances and biological system support with non-developers have truly expanded its reception in the sister orders of information science and logical figuring. Incalculable working analysts, cosmologists, researcher, and business examiners have become Python software engineers and have improved the tooling. Programming is, on a very basic level, a social action, and Python's people group has recognized this more than some other language with the exception of JavaScript.

AI is an especially incorporation substantial order, as in any AI/AI framework is going to need to ingest a lot of information from true sources as preparing information, or framework input, so Python's wide library environment implies that it is regularly well-situated to get to and change that information.

Python enables users to concentrate on genuine issues

Python is exceptionally straightforward for researchers who are regularly not prepared in software engineering. It expels a large number of the complexities that you need to manage when attempting to drive the outer libraries that you have to perform inquire about.

After Numeric (presently NumPy) began the advancement, the expansion of IPython Notebooks (presently Jupyter Notebooks), matplotlib, and numerous different apparatuses to make things significantly increasingly instinctive, Python has enabled researchers to for the most part consider answers for issues and less about the innovation expected to drive these arrangements.

"Python is a perfect reconciliation language which ties advancements together effortlessly."

As in different regions, Python is a perfect reconciliation language, which ties advancements together easily. Python enables users to concentrate on genuine issues, instead of investing energy in usage subtleties. Aside from making things simpler for the user, Python additionally sparkles as a perfect paste stage for the individuals who build up the low-level combinations with outside libraries. This is primarily because of Python being entirely available by means of a decent and extremely complete C API.

Python is extremely simple to use for math and details arranged individuals.

I think there are two principal reasons, which are extremely related. The principal reason is that Python is overly simple to peruse and learn.

I would contend that the vast majority working in AI and AI need to concentrate on evaluating their thoughts in the most advantageous manner conceivable. The emphasis is on research and applications, and programming is only an instrument to get you there. The more agreeable a programming language is to learn, the lower the section hindrance is for more math and details situated individuals.

Python is likewise overly lucid, which causes with staying up with the latest with business as usual in AI and AI, for instance, when perusing code usage of calculations and thoughts. Attempting new thoughts in AI and AI regularly requires executing moderately complex calculations, and the more straightforward the language, the simpler it is to investigate.

The subsequent principal reason is that while Python is a truly open language itself, we have a ton of extraordinary libraries over it that make our work simpler. No one might want to invest their energy in reimplementing fundamental calculations without any preparation (aside from with regards to contemplating AI and AI). The huge number of Python libraries that exist helps us to concentrate on more energizing things than rehashing an already solved problem.

Python is likewise a brilliant wrapper language for working with progressively proficient C/C++ usage of calculations and CUDA/cuDNN, which is the reason existing AI and profound learning libraries run effectively in Python. This is additionally very significant for working in the fields of AI and AI.

To condense, I would state that Python is an extraordinary language that lets specialists and professionals center on AI and AI and gives to a lesser degree an interruption than different language.

Python has such huge numbers of highlights that are appealing for logical registering.

The most significant and quick reason is that the NumPy and SciPy libraries empower undertakings, for example, scikit-realize, which is, as of now, just about a true standard instrument for AI.

The motivation behind why NumPy, SciPy, scikit-learn, thus numerous different libraries were made in any case is on the grounds that Python has a few highlights that make it extremely alluring for logical processing. Python has a straightforward and reliable syntax, which makes programming progressively open to individuals who are not programming engineers.

"Python profits by a rich environment of libraries for logical registering."

Another explanation is operator over-burdening, which empowers code that is clear and succinct. At that point, there's Python's support convention (PEP 3118), which is a standard for outer libraries to interoperate productively with Python when preparing clusters like information structures. At long last, Python profits by a rich biological system of libraries for logical processing, which pulls in more researchers and makes an idealistic cycle.

Python is useful for AI since it is exacting and predictable.

What we're doing in that field is building up our math and calculations. We're putting the calculations that we unquestionably need to keep and streamline into libraries, for example, scikit-learn. At that point, we're proceeding to repeat and share notes on how we sort out and consider the information.

A significant level of scripting language is perfect for AI and AI since we can quickly move things around and attempt once more. The code that we make burns through the vast majority of its lines on speaking to the real math and information structures, not on the standard.

A scripting language like Python is far and away superior since it is severe and reliable. Everybody can see each other's Python code obviously superior to them could work in some other language that has confounding and conflicting programming standards.

The accessibility of instruments like the IPython journal has made it conceivable to repeat and share our math and calculations on an unheard-of level. Python accentuates the center of the work that we're attempting to do and totally limits everything else about how we give the PC guidelines, which is the means by which it ought to be. Robotize whatever you don't should consider.

INSTALLATION

The Installation Tutorial; A Step by Step Complete Guide

Python is a well-known programming language. Actually, you will consider them to be of python language as the English language. The Python 2 and Python 3 are the two significant renditions of Python. Be that as it may, Python Installation for both the adaptations are unique. What's more, Commands and way condition factors for both the renditions are unique. You can pick your python form as indicated by your prerequisite. Fledglings consistently face difficulties in installing Python in their working framework. This article, Python Installation instructional exercise is for them. Prologue to Python Programming article is a finished guide for fledglings to find out about Python. You will realize how to install python in Windows, Linux, macOS. Step by step instructions to check your Python renditions. You try to install python cautiously by perusing every one of the means depicted here else it might be wrongly installed.

Python Installation Tutorial for Windows

In this area, you will realize how to do Python installation in the Windows OS. First, we will cover for the most recent Python 3 form and afterward Python 2 rendition. You can either install both the variants or pick the form, as indicated by your ultimate objective.

Python 3 Major Version Installation

Stage 1 – Download the most recent Python 3.x form. At the hour of composing this article most recent rendition was Python 3.6.4. Download Windows x86 – 64 executable record just as the installer will consequently install 32 or 64 pieces of Python as indicated by the framework configuration.

Python Releases for Windows

- Latest Python 3 Release - Python 3.6.4
- Latest Python 2 Release - Python 2.7.14

- Python 3.6.4 - 2017-12-19
  - Download Windows x86 web-based installer
  - Download Windows x86 executable installer
  - Download Windows x86 embeddable zip file
  - Download Windows x86-64 web-based installer
  - Download Windows x86-64 executable installer
  - Download Windows x86-64 embeddable zip file
  - Download Windows help file

Stage 2 – Open the executable record and Check the Add Python 3.6 to PATH. At that point, click on the Install Now Button. It will show the installation progress.

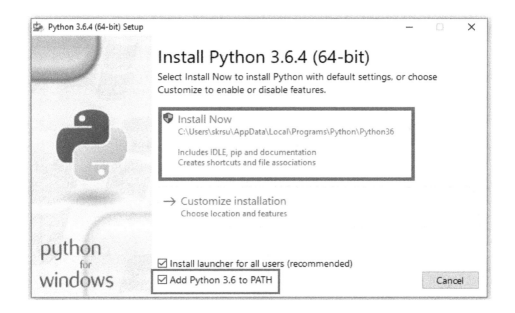

Step 3 – After the installation progress is finished, you will see the Disable way length limit. Presently you should think about what is it, and whats will occur on the off chance that I will incapacitate it. The appropriate response is clear, and it will expel the restrictions on the MAX_PATH variable. It will permit us to utilize long way names for the Python. We prescribe you not to impair this alternative as it will expel any way related issues while working in Windows. In this way, click on the nearby catch to complete the installation.

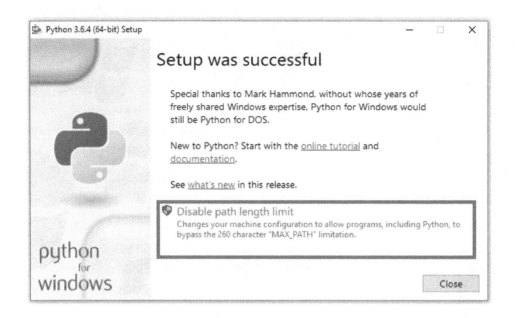

Step 4 – Now, Python 3.6 is installed. You can check it is possible that it is appropriately installed or not. You can do it through Command Prompt. Open the order brief and type the accompanying direction. It will output the form of Python.

Congratulations, you have effectively installed Python 3 form. In the following area, you will realize how to install Python 2.x forms. In the event that you need to know the distinction between Python 3 and Python 2, highlights, and application.

Python 2 Major Version Installation

Step 1 – Download the most recent Python 2.x adaptation. The most recent variant at the hour of composing this article is Python 2.7.14. You can likewise download different forms by looking down. If we prescribe you to download the most recent discharges. Pick the Windows x86-64 MSI installer to install in 32 pieces or 64 piece Windows OS.

- Python 2.7.14 - 2017-09-16
  - Download Windows x86 MSI installer
  - Download Windows x86-64 MSI installer
  - Download Windows help file
  - Download Windows debug information files for 64-bit binaries
  - Download Windows debug information files

Step 2-Run the installer and select install for all users — Snap "Next " catch to proceed.

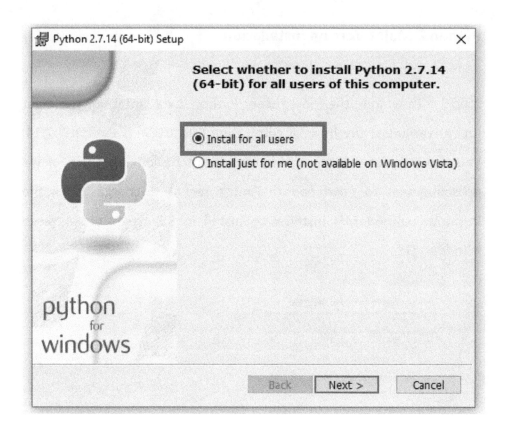

You will see the decision to choose the goal index. Leave for what it's worth and snap the "Following Button."

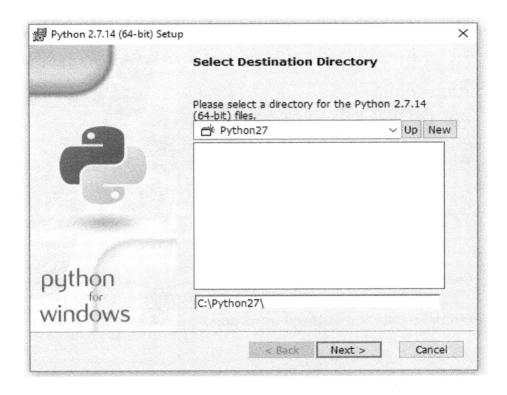

Step 3 – After step 2, you need to do some customization. Look down and click on Add python.exe to way and select "Will be installed on the nearby hard drive." At that point, click on the Next catch to finish the installation progress.

Step 4-The Python 2.7.14 had been installed. Also, you need to check whether it has been appropriately installed or not. You need to utilize a similar after the direction. It will output the python adaptation.

Python - V

```
Command Prompt                                               —  □  ×
Microsoft Windows [Version 10.0.16299.192]
(c) 2017 Microsoft Corporation. All rights reserved.

C:\Users\skrsu>python -V
Python 2.7.14

C:\Users\skrsu>
```

On the off chance that you see the above output, at that point, praise you have effectively install the Python 2.7.14 adaptation.

Python Installation Tutorial for Linux

Linux is an open-source Operating System. There are numerous Linux based working frameworks. Famous are Ubuntu, Fedora, Linux Mint, Debian. In this segment, you will figure out how to do python installation for both Python 3 and Python 2 variants. Fedora Linux OS utilized for Installation of python. The majority of the more current Linux based Operating framework has just installed the Python application. You will then check if it is installed or not by composing the accompanying directions in the terminal.

For Python3

$ python3 - adaptation

For Python2

$ python2 - form

You will consider the to be formed as output like in the underneath screen capture. However, if you do not see, at that point, you need to install Python. Pursue the accompanying steps for effective install.

Open the terminal or Command brief from your Linux based OS. Type the accompanying directions.

On the off chance that you are utilizing Ubuntu 16.0 or more up to date form, at that point, you can without much of a stretch install Python 3.6 or Python 2.7 by composing the accompanying directions.

$ sudo able get update

$ sudo able get install python3.6

$ sudo able get an update

$ sudo able get install python2.7

More current Versions of Fedora have pre-installed both the forms of Python. If you are utilizing other Linux appropriations, there is an increased chance that Python is pre-installed.

Python Installation Tutorial for MacOs

macOS is a working framework created by Apple Inc. It is much the same as the Windows Operating System and another working framework. The greater part of the more current adaptations of MacOS has pre-installed python. You can check whether the python is installed or not by the accompanying directions.

Python - adaptation

Python 3 application or Python 2 Major Version Installation

Download Python 3 or 2 new type. At the hour of composing this post, Python 3.6 or Python 2.7 was the fresher form. Download the

Mac OS X 64-piece/32-piece installer. Run the bundle and following the installation steps to install the python bundles.

Python Releases for Mac OS X

- Latest Python 3 Release - Python 3.6.4
- Latest Python 2 Release - Python 2.7.14

- Python 3.7.0a4 - 2018-01-09
  - Download Mac OS X 64-bit/32-bit installer
- Python 3.6.4 - 2017-12-19
  - Download Mac OS X 64-bit/32-bit installer

Python Releases for Windows

After the effective installation, you can check the python form by utilizing a similar order.

Python - version

Python Installation on Windows, Linux, and MacOS can be a troublesome errand for apprentices. Actually, You need to pursue the installation steps for fruition painstakingly. The above steps for the python installation must be pursued for fruitful installing. Else, it might lead error, and you will incapable of discovering Python Version when you beware of direction brief. I trust this article probably settled your question about how to do python installation. In any case, Don't neglect to buy in our blog for a most recent post on the Python programming language. Additionally, You may compose proposals and remark in remark box beneath.

NUMBERS

Python numbers are a gathering of four information types: plain whole number, long whole number, coasting point, and complex numbers. They bolster basic number-crunching estimations as well as be utilized in the quantum calculation as mind-boggling numbers.

Python has three unmistakable numeric types: whole numbers, skimming point numbers, and complex numbers. These are typically alluded to as int, skim, and complex types. Additionally, the boolean type is a subtype of the number type.

int

Alludes to a whole number. A number is an entire number (for example, not a part). Whole numbers can be a positive number, a negative one, or zero. Instances of whole numbers: - 3, - 2, - 1, 0, 1, 2, 3

float

Alludes to a floating point number. Skimming point numbers speak to genuine numbers and are composed with a decimal point partitioning the whole number and the fragmentary parts. Skimming point numbers can likewise be in logical documentation, with E or e showing the intensity of 10 (e.g., +1e3 is identical to 1000.0). Instances of buoys: 1.0, 12.45, 10.4567, - 10.0, - 20.76789, 64.2e18, - 64.2e18.

complex

An intricate number takes the structure a + bj where a will be a genuine number, and b is a fanciful number. Every contention a be any numeric type (counting complex). The primary contention can likewise be a string (yet the subsequent contention can't). Models: 1.4j, - 1.4j, 2+18j, - 2.18j, 5.14-7j, 5.14e+45j, - 5.14e+45j.

In Python, every numeric type is permanent. I you need to change any piece of a number, you have to reassign the number itself.

Python Numbers, Type Conversion, and Mathematics

Python Numbers – Types Of Numeric Data

Strangely, Python 2.x had four worked in information types (int, long, buoy, and complex) to speak to numbers. Later, Python 3.x evacuated the long and stretched out the int type to have boundless length.

The Int Type

The int type speaks to the principal whole number information type in Python. The plain number in Python 2.x had the most extreme size up to the value of sys.maxint.

While in 3.x, the int type got elevated to have boundless length and, in this manner, disposed of the long.

```
>>> x = 9

>>> type(x)

<type 'int'>
```

The Long Type

A whole number with boundless length. Until the finish of Python 2.x, the numbers were permitted to flood and transformed into a along. This conduct changed since 3.0, where the ints supplanted the aches.

```
>>> x = 9999999999
```

```
>>> type(x) # In Python 2.x, the type will belong. While in 3.x, it is int independent of the size.
```

```
<type 'long'>
```

The Float Type

The buoy speaks to a paired gliding point number. Utilizing a buoy variable in an articulation naturally changes over the connecting yearns and ints to drifts.

```
>>> x = 9.999
```

```
>>> type(x)
```

```
<type 'float'>
```

The Complex Type

The number of this type has a genuine and nonexistent part. For instance – The articulation (n1 + n2j) speaks to an intricate type where both n1 and n2 are the drifting point numbers indicating the genuine and nonexistent parts separately.

```
>>> x = 3 + 4j
```

```
>>> type(x)
<class 'complex'>
>>> x.real
3.0
>>> x.imag
4.0
```

Python Numbers – Key Points

1.

1. The number types are consequently upcast in the accompanying request.

Int → Long → Float → Complex

2. While whole numbers in Python 3.x can be of any length, a buoy type number is just exact to fifteen decimal spots.

3. Usually, we work with numbers dependent on the decimal (base 10) number framework. However, attimes, we may need to utilize other number frameworks, for example, twofold (base 2), hexadecimal (base 16), and octal (base 8).

In Python, we can arrange such numbers utilizing the best possible prefixes. See underneath.

Number System

Base

Prefix to Use

Double

Base-2

'0b' or '0B'

Octal

Base-8

'0o' or '0O'

Hex

Base-16

'0x' or '0X'

```
>>> x = 0b101
>>> print(x)
```

5

```
>>> type(x)
<type 'int'>
>>> print(0b101 + 5)


10


>>> print(0o123)
83
>>> type(0x10)
<type 'int'>
```

4. If you need to test the class type of a number in Python, at that point, you should utilize the instance() function.

isinstance(object, class)

Here is the model.

```
>>> isinstance(2.2, coast)


Genuine
```

5. If you utilize blended information types in an articulation, at that point, all operands will go to carry on as the most mind-boggling type utilized.

6. >>> 2 + 3.8

5.8

7. Be cautious while separating numbers in Python.

In Python 2.x, the division (/) will restore a whole number remainder as the output.

8. >>> 7/2

3

In Python 3.x, the division (/) will restore a buoy remainder as the output.

>>> 7/2

3.5

9. The floor operator (//) restores the whole number remainder, and the mod (%) operator gives the rest of. In any case, you can get both these by utilizing the divmod() function.

10. >>> divmod(7, 2)

11. (3, 1)

12. >>> 7 % 2

13. 1

14. >>> 7/2

15. 3.5

16. >>> 7/2

3

Type Conversion (Casting) In Python

In Python, it is truly simple to change over any numeric information type into another. We call this procedure as intimidation in Pythonic terms.

Essential tasks, for example, expansion, and subtraction constrain number to glide certainly (as a matter of course) on the off chance that one of the operands is a buoy.

>>> 2 + 4.5

6.5

In the above model, the whole main number (2) transformed into a buoy (2.0) for expansion, and the output is additionally a gliding point number.

Be that as it may, Python spreads out a no. of inherent functions, for example, int(), buoy(), and complex() to change over between types unequivocally. These functions can even change over strings to numbers.

>>> int(3.7)

3

```
>>> int(- 3.4)
```

- 3

```
>>> float(3)
```

3.0

```
>>> complex(4 + 7j)
```

(4+7j)

If you don't mind note that on the off chance that you are doing a transformation of a buoy to whole number, at that point the number will get shortened (i.e., the whole number which is near zero).

External Classes to Handle Python Numbers

As you've perused over that Python's worked in glide class has the utmost to control accuracy up to the fifteen decimal spots. Notwithstanding, there are different impediments also in light of the fact that it completely relies upon the PC usage of the gliding point numbers. For instance, see the beneath decimal point issue.

```
>>> 1.1 + 3.2
```

4.300000000000001

To conquer such type of issues, we can utilize the decimal module in Python.

Python Decimal

The decimal module gives the fixed and drifting point number juggling usage, which is natural to the vast majority. Dissimilar to the coasting point numbers, which have exactness up to 15 decimal places, the decimal module acknowledges a user-characterized value. It can even protect huge digits in a no.

```
import decimal
print(0.28)
print(decimal.Decimal(0.28))
print(decimal.Decimal('5.30'))
```

```
Output-
0.28
0.2800000000000000266453525910037569701671600341796875
5.30
```

Python Fractions
Python bundles a module named as 'portions,' to deal with partial numbers.
A portion consolidates a numerator and a denominator; both are of whole number information type. This module empowers discerning number math functionality.

Here is a straightforward guide to make and utilize part type objects.

```
import portions
print(fractions.Fraction(2.5))
print(fractions.Fraction(5.2))
print(fractions.Fraction(3,5))
print(fractions.Fraction(1.3))
print(fractions.Fraction('3.7'))
```

Output-

5/2

5854679515581645/1125899906842624

3/5

5854679515581645/4503599627370496

37/10

With the assistance of Python numbers and the math module, you can do any essential to cutting edge calculations in Python. We trust this instructional exercise would have the option to inspire your learning spirits.

THE PHYTON NUMBER TYPES –

Python Int, Float, Complex Numbers

1. Python Number Types

Presently, we will dive somewhat more profound into those Python programming number types. A python number can be-Python int, Python drift, or even Python complex number. Long is never again bolstered by Python 3.x.

Python Number Types – The Python Int, Float, Complex Numbers

2. Python Number Types

Before beginning with Python number types in, let us change Python essentials and different syntax utilized in Python for better understanding.

A number is a number-crunching substance that lets us measure something. Python enables us to store the whole number, skimming, and complex numbers, and furthermore lets us convert between them. Since Python is progressively typed, there is no compelling reason to determine the type of information for a variable. So now we should begin with python number types.

• None-The None watchword demonstrates the nonappearance of value.

3. Python int

Python can hold marked numbers.

1. >>> a=7

2. >>> a

7

It have the ability to hold a value of any length, the main confinement being the measure of memory accessible.

1. >>> a=99999999999999999999999999999999999

2. >>> a

99999999999999999999999999999999999

There are three types of Python number types:

Python Number Types – Python Int

I. type() function

It takes one contention, and returns which class it has a place with.

1. >>> a=9999999999999999999999999999999999999

2. >>> type(a)

<class 'int'>

ii. isinstance() function

It takes two contentions. The first is the construct(ex-a variable or a list), and the second is a class. It returns True or False and this depends on whether the developer has a place with that class. Assume we need to check if 'a' has a place with class bool. We compose the accompanying code for the equivalent.

1. >>> isinstance(a,bool)

Bogus

Since it has a place with the class 'int' rather, it returns False.

iii. Exponential numbers

You can compose an exponential number utilizing the letter 'e' between the mantissa and the example.

1. >>> print(2e5)

200000.0

Recollect this is the intensity of 10. To raise a number to another's capacity, we utilize the ** operator.

In the event that you face trouble in Python number types, if it's not too much trouble remark.

4. Python drift

Python additionally bolsters coasting point genuine values. An int can't store the value of the scientific consistent pi. However, a buoy can.

```
1. >>> from math import pi

2. >>> pi

3.141592653589793

1. >>> type(pi)

<class 'float'>
```

A buoy value is just exact up to 15 decimal spots. From that point onward, it adjusts the number.

```
1. >>> a=1.1111111111111111119

2. >>> a

1.1111111111111112
```

Note that division brings about buoys.

1. >>> 2/2

1.0

5. Python Complex Numbers

A mind-boggling number is a Python number type made of genuine and fanciful parts. It is spoken to as a+bj.

1. >>> a=2+3j

2. >>> a

(2+3j)

I. Coefficient to the nonexistent part

Here, 2 is the genuine part, and 3j is the nonexistent part. To indicate the unreasonable part, notwithstanding, you can't utilize the letter 'I' as you would do on paper.

1. >>> a=2+3i

SyntaxError: invalid syntax

Additionally, it is required to give a coefficient to the nonexistent part.

1. >>> a=2+j

Traceback (latest call last):

Document "<pyshell#33>", line 1, in <module>

a=2+j

NameError: name 'j' isn't characterized

For this situation, a coefficient of 1 will do.

1. >>> a=2+1j

2. >>> a

(2+1j)

ii. Tasks on complex numbers

At long last, you can play out the fundamental tasks on complex numbers as well.

1. >>> a=2+3j

2. >>> b=2+5j

3. >>> a+b

(4+8j)

1. >>> a*=2

2. >>> a

(4+6j)

Here, *= is a setup task operator.

Any Doubt yet in Python number Type? If it's not too much trouble, Comment.

6. Composing numbers in twofold, octal, and hexadecimal

As a rule, developers need to manage numbers other than decimal. To do this, you can utilize proper prefixes.

Number System Prefix

Binary 0b or 0B

Octal 0o or 0O

Hexadecimal 0x or 0X

I. Parallel

At the point when you need to compose a parallel number, utilize the prefix 0b or 0B. For instance, we realize that the paired for 7 is 111.

1. >>> print(0b111)

7

You can likewise apply transformation functions on these numbers.

1. >>> int(0b10).

2

ii. The Octal.

This prefix is assigned for octal is 0o or 0O.

1. >>> print(0O10)

8

The accompanying code causes an error. This is on the grounds that the octal number framework doesn't have the number 8. It has the numbers 0-7.

1. >>> print(0O8)

SyntaxError: invalid token

1. >>> float(0B10)

2.0

iii. Hexadecimal

The hexadecimal number framework has numbers 0-9 and afterward, A-F. For that, utilization of the prefix 0x or 0X.

1. >>> print(0xFF)

255

1. >>> print(0xFE)

254

7. Python Conversion Functions

Albeit most occasions, Python does the change varying, and you can do it unequivocally on the off chance that you need. These functions enable us to change over one numeric type into another python number type.

Python Number Types – Python Conversion Functions

I. int()

The int() function can change over another numeric type into an int. It can likewise change over different types into an int, yet in this instructional exercise, we center around numeric types.

1. >>> int(7)

7

1. >>> int(7.7)

7

As should be obvious, it doesn't adjust the number 7.7 up to 8; it shortens the 0.7.

In any case, you can't change over an intricate number into an int.

1. >>> int(2+3j)

Traceback (latest call last):

Record "<pyshell#22>", line 1, in <module>

int(2+3j)

TypeError: can't change over complex to int

1. >>> int(3j)

Traceback (latest call last):

Record "<pyshell#23>", line 1, in <module>

int(3j)

TypeError: can't change over complex to int

We can likewise apply this function on portrayals other than decimal, i.e., paired, octal, and hexadecimal.

1. >>> int(0b10)

2

1. >>> int(0xF)

15

ii. drift()

This function changes over another numeric type into a buoy.

1. >>> float(110)

110.0

1. >>> float(110.0)

110.0

Like int(), skim() can't change over a complex either.

1. >>> float(3j)

Traceback (latest call last):

Record "<pyshell#26>", line 1, in <module>

float(3j)

TypeError: can't change over complex to glide
1. >>> float(0o10).

8.0

Here, we can apply it to an octal number.

iii. complex()

The complex() function changes over another numeric type into a complex number.

1. >>> complex(2)

(2+0j)

1. >>> complex(2.3)

(2.3+0j)

1. >>> complex(2+3.0j)

(2+3j)

iv. receptacle()

The receptacle() function restores the parallel value of a number.

1. >>> bin(2)

'0b10'

In any case, you can't have any significant bearing it to a buoy value or a complex value. The equivalent is valid for oct() and hex() functions as well.

1. >>> bin(2.3)

Traceback (latest call last):

Record "<pyshell#49>", line 1, in <module>

bin(2.3)

TypeError: 'glide' object can't be deciphered as a whole number.

1. >>> bin(2+3j)

Traceback (latest call last):

Record "<pyshell#50>", line 1, in <module>

bin(2+3j)

TypeError: 'complex' object can't be translated as a whole number.

v. oct()

This function restores the octal value of a number.

1. >>> oct(8)

'0o10'

We realize that 8.0 is equivalent to 8; however the function doesn't think the equivalent. It is a buoy, so it can't change over it into oct.

1. >>> oct(8.0)

Traceback (latest call last):

Record "<pyshell#59>", line 1, in <module>

oct(8.0)

TypeError: 'glide' object can't be deciphered as a whole number.

vi. hex()

The hex() function restores the hexadecimal value of a number.

1. >>> hex(255)

'0xff'

1. >>> hex(0)

'0x0'

1. >>> hex(0)

'0x0'

8. Python Decimal Module

How about we give a shot including 1.1 and 2.2 in the shell, and we should contrast it and 3.3.

1. >>> (1.1+2.2)==3.3

Bogus

For what reason did it return False? We should take a stab at printing the whole.

1. >>> 1.1+2.2

3.3000000000000003

Woah, how did this occur? Indeed, this is appropriately credited to equipment constraints and isn't a defect of Python. Since the home improvement shops decimals as twofold parts, it is beyond the realm of imagination to expect to store it precisely. How about we take a model.

1. >>> 1/3

0.3333333333333333

At the point when we isolate 1 by 3, it doesn't restore the full value, which is 0.3333333333333333... Python provides an answer to this issue. It has the 'decimal' module, which lets us pick accuracy. We will find out about modules in a later exercise.

1. >>> import decimal

2. >>> print(decimal.Decimal(0.1))

0.1000000000000000055511151231257827021181583404541015625

Did you see what occurred here? The Decimal() function saved the significance. This was the Decimal Function Python number type.

9. The parts Module

Another module that Python gives the parts module lets you manage divisions. The Fraction() function restores the value as numerator and denominator.

1. >>> from divisions import Fraction

2. >>> print(Fraction(1.5))

3/2

It can likewise take two contentions.

1. >>> print(Fraction(1,3))

1/3

10. The math Module

Another basic module is the math module. It has exceedingly significant scientific functions like exp, trigonometric functions, logarithmic functions, factorial, and that's only the tip of the iceberg.

1. >>> import math

2. >>> math.factorial(5)

120

1. >>> math.exp(3)

20.085536923187668

1. >>> math.tan(90)

- 1.995200412208242

This was about the Python number types.

FUNCTIONS

What are the Functions?

Functions are a helpful method to partition your code into valuable squares, enabling us to arrange our code, make it increasingly meaningful, reuse it and spare some time. Likewise, functions are a key method to characterize interfaces so software engineers can share their code.

Functions are a major piece of Python (and most other programming language). Python remembers an enormous number of worked for functions, yet you can likewise make your own functions.

A function ordinarily plays out a particular errand that you can run in your program. For instance, print() is a work in Python function that enables you to show content to the screen. Calling print("Hey") results in Hey being shown.

An incredible aspect concerning functions is that they can be utilized as a "black box." You don't have to know how the function is coded so as to utilize it. Truth be told, you don't have to see the function code before utilizing it. All you have to know is the manner by which to call the function.

You call a function by alluding in its possession and giving any contentions that it may require. So calling print("Hey") calls the print() function and passes a contention of "Hello".

You can likewise make your own functions. This empowers you to make code that can be reused again and again. The code inside the function doesn't really run until you call the function.

Worked In Python Functions

Before you choose to plunk down and compose an awesome function, ask yourself, "is there effectively a form in function for this?".

Python incorporates a number of functions incorporated right with the mediator that you can utilize straight away. Now and then you may find that there's as of now a function that does what you need, or if nothing else part of it.

For instance, Python incorporates a total() function that could be utilized rather than calculation.sum that we utilized in the above model. Actually, the inherent sum()function accomplishes more, as it enables you to give a list of numbers (for example, it can include multiple numbers one after another).

The accompanying functions are constantly accessible, as they're assembled directly into the Python translator. In case you're acquainted with other programming language, you'll likely perceive a portion of these and think about how they work. Regardless, see the official docs for more data about how everyone functions.

- abs()
- all()
- any()
- ascii()
- bin()
- bool()
- bytearray()
- bytes()
- callable()
- chr()
- classmethod()
- compile()
- complex()
- delattr()

- dict()
- dir()
- divmod()
- enumerate()
- eval()
- exec()
- filter()
- float()
- format()
- frozenset()
- getattr()
- globals()
- hasattr()
- hash()
- help()
- hex()
- id()
- input()
- int()
- isinstance()
- issubclass()
- iter()
- len()
- list()

- locals()
- map()
- max()
- memoryview()
- min()
- next()
- object()
- oct()
- open()
- ord()
- pow()
- print()
- property()
- range()
- repr()
- reversed()
- round()
- set()
- setattr()
- slice()
- sorted()

- staticmethod()

- str()

- sum()

- super()

- tuple()

- type()

- vars()

- zip()

- __import__()

The Python Functions – A Step by Step Guide for Beginners

This instructional exercise strolls you through the idea of Python function. It encourages you to figure out how to make user-characterized functions and use them to compose particular projects in Python.

A function is an autonomous and reusable square of code which you can consider any no. of times from wherever in a program. It is a fundamental apparatus for developers to part a major task into littler modules.

Functions are the center structure squares of any programming language that a software engineer must figure out how to utilize. Python gives a no. of implicit techniques for direct use and furthermore permits to characterize your custom functions.

Allows now quickly observe what are you going to gain from this instructional exercise.

A function in Python programm is a logical unit of code containing a grouping of statements indented under a name given utilizing the "def" watchword.

Functions enable you to make a logical division of a major undertaking into littler modules. They make your code increasingly reasonable and extensible.

While programming, it keeps you from including copy code and advances reusability.

Step by step instructions to make A Function : Syntax

The syntax of a Python function is because of the following.

Single line function:

```
def single_line(): statement
```

Python function with docstring:

```
def fn(arg1, arg2,...):
```

"""docstring"""

statement1

statement2

Settled Python function:

```
def fn(arg1, arg2,...):
```

"""docstring"""

```
statement1

statement2

def fn_new(arg1, arg2,...):

statement1

statement2

...

...
```

Def Statement

If there is much trouble, read the beneath notes before making your first Python function.

♣ The "def" watchword is a statement for characterizing a function in Python.

♣ You start a function with the def watchword, indicate a name pursued by a colon (:) sign.

♣ The "def" call makes the function object and doles out it to the name given.

♣ You can assist in re-appoint a similar function item to different names.

♣ Give an extraordinary name to your function and adhere to indistinguishable guidelines from naming the identifiers.

♣ Add an important docstring to clarify what the function does. Notwithstanding, it is a discretionary step.

♣ Now, start the function body by including legitimate Python statements, each indented with four spaces.

♣ You can likewise add a statement to restore a value toward the finish of a function. Be that as it may, this step is discretionary.

♣ Just press enter and expel the indentation to end a function.

♣ Since the def is a statement, so you can utilize it anyplace a statement can show up –, for example, settled in an if the condition or inside another function.

Model :

on the off chance that test:

def test(): # First definition

...

else:

def test(): # Alternate definition

...

...

How To Call A Function In Python?

By utilizing the def watchword, you figured out how to make the plan of a function that has a name, parameters to pass, and a body with substantial Python statements.

The subsequent stage is to execute it. You can do as such by calling it from the Python content or inside a function or straightforwardly from the Python shell.

To call a function, you have to determine the function name with applicable parameters, and that is it.

Pursue the beneath guide to figure out how to call a function in Python.

Case Of A Function Call

It's a straightforward model where a function "typeOfNum()" has settled functions to choose a number is either odd or even.

```
def typeOfNum(num): # Function header

# Function body

if that num % 2 == 0:
```

```python
def message():

    print("You entered a much number.")

else:

    def message():

    print("You entered an odd number.")

    message()

# End of function

typeOfNum(2) # call the function

typeOfNum(3) # call the function once more
```

Polymorphism In Python

In Python, functions polymorphism is conceivable as we don't determine the contention types while making functions.

♣ The conduct of a function may fluctuate contingent on the contentions that went to it.

♣ The same function can acknowledge the contentions of various item types.

♣ If the articles locate a coordinating interface, the function can process them.

♣ Python is a progressively typed language that implies the types connect with values, not with factors. Thus, the polymorphism runs unlimited.

♣ That's one of the essential contrasts among Python and other statically typed language, for example, C++ or Java.

♣ In Python, you don't need to make reference to the particular information types while coding.

♣ However, if you do, at that point, as far as possible to the types foreseen at the hour of coding.

♣ Such code won't permit other good types that may require later on.

♣ Python doesn't bolster any type of function over-burdening.

Parameters In A Function

We frequently utilize the parameters and contentions of the term reciprocally. There is a slight contrast between them.

Parameters are the factors utilized in the function definition, while contentions are the values we go to the function parameters.

Python bolsters various varieties of passing parameters to a function. Before we talk about every one of them, you should peruse the accompanying notes.

- o The contention gets allocated to the nearby factor name once went to the function.

- o Changing the value of contention inside a function doesn't influence the guest.

- If the contention holds a variable article, at that point, transforming it in a function impacts the guest.

- We call the death of unchanging contentions as Pass by Value since Python doesn't enable them to change set up.

- The going of impermanent contentions happens to be Pass by Pointer in Python since they are probably going to be influenced by the progressions inside a function.

Watchword Based Arguments

At the point when you dole out value to the parameter (for example, param=value) and go to the function (like fn(param=value)), at that point, it transforms into a catchphrase contention.

On the off chance that you pass the watchword contentions to a function, at that point, Python decides it through the parameter name utilized in the task.

See the beneath model.

def fn(value):

```
print(value)

return

fn(value=123) # output => 123

fn(value="Python!") # output => Python!
```

While utilizing watchword contentions, you should ensure that the name in the task should coordinate with the one in the function definition. Something else, Python tosses the TypeError as demonstrated as follows.

```
fn(value1="Python!") # wrong name utilized in the catchphrase contention
```

The above function consider causes the accompanying error.

```
TypeError: fn() got a sudden watchword contention 'value1'
```

Contentions With Default Values

Python functions permit setting the default values for parameters in the function definition. We allude them as the default contentions.

The callee utilizes these default values when the guest doesn't pass them in the function call.

The beneath model will help you unmistakably comprehend the idea of default contentions.

```python
def daysInYear(is_leap_year=False):

if not is_leap_year:

print("365 days")

else:

print("366 days")

return

daysInYear()

daysInYear(True)
```

Here, the parameter "is_leap_year" is filling in as a default contention. In the event that you don't pass any value, at that point, it accepts the default, which is False.

The output of the above code is:

365 days

366 days

Variable Arguments

You may experience circumstances when you need to pass extra contentions to a Python function. We allude them as factor length contentions.

The Python's print() is itself a case of such a function which bolsters variable contentions.

To characterize a function with variable contentions, you have to prefix the parameter with a reference mark (*) sign. Pursue the beneath syntax.

```python
def fn([std_args,] *var_args_tuple ):

    """docstring"""

    function_body

    return_statement
```

Look at the underneath model for better clearness.

```python
def inventory(category, *items):

    print("%s [items=%d]:" % (class, len(items)), things)

    for thing in things:

        print("- ", thing)

    return

inventory('Electronics', 'television', 'lcd', 'air conditioning', 'cooler', 'radiator')

inventory('Books', 'python', 'java', 'c', 'c++')
```

The output of the above code goes this way.

Hardware [items=5]: ('television', 'lcd', 'air conditioning', 'cooler', 'radiator')

- television

- lcd

- air conditioning

- cooler

- radiator

Books [items=four]: ('python', 'java', 'c', 'c++')

: python

: java

:c

: c++

It will be ideal if you note that you can decide to have a proper contention or not in the function definition alongside the variable contentions.

You may decide to avoid the variable contentions while calling the function. In such a case, the tuple would stay vacant.

Local Variables Inside A Function

A local variable has permeability just inside a code square, for example, the function def.

They are accessible just while the function is executing.

Look at the beneath case of utilizing nearby factors.

def fn(a, b) :

temp = 1

for iter in range(b) :

```
temp = temp*a
```

```
return temp
```

```
print(fn(2, 4))
```

```
print(temp) # error : can not get to 'temp' out of extent of function
'fn'
```

```
print(iter) # error : can not get to 'iter' out of extent of function 'fn'
```

In this model, we attempt to get to nearby factors outside the function body, which brings about the NameError.

Function's nearby factors don't hold values between calls. The names utilized inside a def don't strife with factors outside the def, regardless of whether you've utilized similar names somewhere else.

The variables in python assignment can occur at three different places.
§ Inside a def – it is local to that function
§ In an enclosing def – it is nonlocal to the nested functions
§ Outside all def(s) – it is global to the entire file

Global Variables In A Function

The global watchword is a statement in Python. It empowers variable (names) to hold changes that live outside a def, at the top degree of a module record.

In a solitary global statement, you can determine at least one name isolated by commas.

All the listed names append to the encasing module's extension when allowed or referenced inside the function body.

Check the underneath model.

x = 5

y = 55

def fn() :

global x

x = [3, 7]

y = [1, 33, 55]

```
# a nearby 'y' is allowed and made here

# though, 'x' alludes to the global (name):
fn()
print(x, y)
```

In the programm above, 'x' is a global variable that will hold any adjustment in its value made in the function. Another variable 'y' has a nearby extension and won't convey forward the change.

How about we presently perceive how a globally pronounced name acts in two diverse Python functions.

```
foo = 99


def fn1() :


foo = 'new' # new neighborhood foo made


def fn2() :


global foo
```

```
foo = 'update' # value of global foo changes
```

In the following model, how about we perceive how global carries on with the import statement.

Here, we have the accompanying three contents:

♣ mod_global.py: It includes the global definition and a function changing and showing values.

♣ test1.py: It imports the principal document and gets to the global variable.

♣ test2.py: It is utilizing the "from" statement to import the principal document and getting to the global variable.

```
# mod_global.py

def fn1() :

global x

x = [1,2] ; y = [20, 200]
```

```
# a nearby 'y' is made – available only inside 'f1'

# 'x' can be gotten to anyplace after a call to 'f1'

fn1()

attempt :

print(x, y) # name 'y' isn't characterized – error

but Exception as ex:

print('y - >', ex)

print('x - >', x)

# test1.py

Import mod_global

print('test1 - >', mod_global.x)

# test2.py
```

```
from mod_global import *
```

```
print('test2 - >', x)
```

Name Resolution ina Python Function

It is fundamental to see how to name goals functions in the event of a def statement.

Here are a couple of focuses you should remember.

- o The name assignments make or change nearby names.

- o The LEGB rule comes in the image for looking through the name reference.

- o local – L

- o then encasing functions (assuming any) – E

- o next comes the global – G

- o and the last one is the implicit – B

To acquire understanding, go through the underneath model.

```
#var = 5

def fn1() :

#var = [3, 5, 7, 9]

def fn2() :

#var = (21, 31, 41)

print(var)

fn2()

fn1() # uncomment var assignments individually and check the
output

print(var)
```

Subsequent to uncommenting the principal "var" task, the output is:

5

5

Next, subsequent to uncommenting the second "var" task also, the output is:

[3, 5, 7, 9]

5

At long last, i we uncomment the last "var" task, at that point, the outcome is as per the following.

(21, 31, 41)

5

Extension Lookup In Functions

Python functions can get to names in all accessible encasing def statements.

Check the beneath model.

```
X = 101 # global degree name - unused

def fn1():

X = 102 # Enclosing def nearby

def fn2():

print(X) # Reference made in settled def

fn2() # Prints 102: encasing def nearby

fn1()
```

The extension query stays in real life regardless of whether the encasing function has just returned.

```
def fn1():

print('In fn1')

X = 100

def fn2():
```

```
print('In fn2')

print(X) # Remembers X in encasing def scope

return fn2 # Return fn2 yet don't call it

movement = fn1() # Make, return work

movement() # Call fn2() directly: prints 100
```

The yield is according to the accompanying.

```
In fn1

In fn2

100
```

The output is as per the following.

```
In fn1

In fn2
```

100

Return Values From A Python Function

In Python functions, you can include the "arrival" statement to restore value.

For the most part, the functions return a solitary value. In any case, whenever required, Python permits restoring various values by utilizing the assortment types, for example, utilizing a tuple or list.

This element works like the call-by-reference by returning tuples and doling out the outcomes back to the first contention names in the caller.

```
def returnDemo(val1, val2) :

val1 = 'Windows'

val2 = 'working framework X'

return val1, val2 # return various characteristics in a tuple
```

```
var1 = 4

var2 = [2, 4, 6, 8]

print("before return =>", var1, var2)

var1, var2 = returnDemo(var1, var2)

print("after return =>", var1, var2)
```

The above code gives the going with yield.

```
before return => 4 [2, 4, 6, 8]

after return => Windows OS XTOC
```

Function Examples

General Function

Look at a general function call model.

```
def getMin(*varArgs) :
```

```
min = varArgs[0]

for I in varArgs[1:] :

    in the event that I < min :

        min = I

    return min

min = getMin(21, - 11, 17, - 23, 6, 5, - 89, 4, 9)

print(min)
```

The output is as per the following.

```
- 89
```

Recursive Function

Next is a case of the recursive function.

```
def calcFact(num) :
```

```python
if(num != 1) :

return num * calcFact(num-1)

else :

return 1

print(calcFact(4))
```

The output is as per the following.

```
24
```

TOC

Python Functions As Objects

Indeed, Python treats everything as an item, and functions are the same.

You can allot a function article to some other names.

```python
def testFunc(a, b) : print('testFunc called')
```

```
fn = testFunc

fn(22, 'bb')
```

The output is:

```
testFunc called
```

You can even pass the function item to different functions as indicated

```
def fn1(a, b, c) : print('fn1 called')

def fn2(fun, x, y, z) : fun(x, y, z)

fn2(fn1, 22, 'bb')
```

The output is:

```
fn1 called
```

You can likewise install a function object in information structures.

```
def fn1(a) : print('fn1', a)
```

```
def fn2(a) : print('fn2', a)
```

```
listOfFuncs = [(fn1, "First function"), (fn2, "Second function")]
```

```
for (f, arg) in listOfFuncs : f(arg)
```

The output is:

fn1 First function

fn2 Second function

You can restore a function object from another function.

```
def FuncLair(produce) :
```

```
def fn1() : print('fn1 called')
```

```
def fn2() : print('fn2 called')
```

```
def fn3() : print('fn3 called')
if that produce == 1 : return fn1
```

```
elif produce == 2 : return fn2
else : return fn3
f = FuncLair(2) ; f()
```

The output is:

```
fn2 called
```

Function Attributes

Python functions additionally have characteristics.

- You can list them by means of the dir() worked in function.
- The traits can be a framework characterized.
- Some of them can be user-characterized also.
- The dir() function additionally lists the user-characterized characteristics.

You can use the function credits to file state data as opposed to utilizing any of the globals or nonlocals names.

Dissimilar to the nonlocals, traits are available anyplace the function itself is, even from outside its code.

OPERATORS

The Python Operators – Types of Operators in Python

Python Operator – Objective

Python operator is an image that plays out an activity on at least one operand. An operand is a variable and a value on that we play out the activity.

The Python OperatorProgramm – Types of Operators in Python

Prologue to Python Operator

Python Operator falls into 7 classes:

- Python Arithmetic Operator

- Python Relational Operator

- Python Assignment Operator

- Python Logical Operator

- Python Membership Operator

- Python Identity Operator

- Python Bitwise Operator

Python Arithmetic Operator

These Python number juggling operators incorporate Python operators for fundamental numerical activities.

Number-crunching Operators in Python

a. Addition(+)

Includes the values either side of the operator.

1. >>> 3+4

Output: 7

b. Subtraction(-)

Subtracts the value on the privilege from the one on the left.

1. >>> 3-4

Output: - 1

c. Multiplication(*)

Duplicates the values on either side of the operator.

1. >>> 3*4

Output: 12

d. Division(/)

Partitions the value on the left by the one on the right. Notice that division brings about a drifting point value.

1. >>> 3/4

Output: 0.75

e. Exponentiation(**)

Raises the principal number to the intensity of the second.

1. >>> 3**4

Output: 81

f. Floor Division(//)

Partitions and returns the numeric value of the remainder. It-dumps the digits after the decimal.

1. >>> 3//4

2. >>> 4//3

Output: 1

1. >>> 10//3

Output: 3

g. Modulus(%)

Partitions and returns the value of the rest.

1. >>> 3%4

Output: 3

1. >>> 4%3

Output: 1

1. >>> 10%3

Output: 1

1. >>> 10.5%3

Output: 1.5

In the event that you face any question in Python Operator with models, ask us in the remark.

Python Relational Operator

Social Python Operator completes the examination between operands. They disclose to us whether an operand is more prominent than the other, lesser, equivalent, or a mix of those.

a. Less than(<) sign

This operator check wether the value on the left of the operator is lesser than the one on the right.

1. >>> 3<4

Output: True

b. GREATER than (>) SIGN

It checks wether the value on the left of the operator is more prominent than the one on the right.

1. >>> 3>4

Output: False

c. Not exactly or equivalent to(<=)

It will check if the value on the left of the operator is lesser than or equivalent to the one on the right.

1. >>> 7<=7

Output: True

d. More noteworthy than or equivalent to(>=)

It will check if the value on the left of the operator is more noteworthy than or equivalent to the one on the right.

1. >>> 0>=0

Output: True

e. Equivalent to(= =)

This operator checks wether the value on the left of the operator is equivalent to the one on the right. 1 is equivalent to the Boolean value True. However, 2 isn't. Additionally, 0 is equivalent to False.

1. >>> 3==3.0

Output: True

1. >>> 1==True

Output: True

1. >>> 7==True

Output: False

1. >>> 0==False

Output: True

1. >>> 0.5==True

Output: False

f. Not rise to to(!=)

It checks wether the value on the left of the operator isn't equivalent to the one on the right. The Python operator <> does likewise work, yet has been relinquished in Python 3.

At the point when the condition for a relative operator is satisfied, it returns True. Else, it returns False. You can utilize this arrival value in a further statement or articulation.

1. >>> 1!=1.0

Output: False

1. >>> - 1<>-1.0

#This causes a syntax error

Python Assignment Operator

Task Python Operator clarified –

A task operator appoints a value to a variable. It might control the value by a factor before allotting it. We have 8 task operators-one plain, and seven for the 7 number-crunching python operators.

a. Assign(=)

Relegates a value to the articulation on the left. Notice that = is utilized for looking at, yet = is utilized for relegating.

1. >>> a=7

2. >>> print(a)

Output: 7

b. Include and Assign(+=)

Includes the values either side and relegates it to the articulation on the left. a+=10 is equivalent to a=a+10.

The equivalent goes for all the following task operators.

1. >>> a+=2

2. >>> print(a)

Output: 9

c. Subtract and Assign(- =)

Subtracts the value on the privilege from the value on the left. At that point, it allocates it to the articulation on the left.

1. >>> a-=2

2. >>> print(a)

Output: 7

d. Partition and Assign(/=)

Partitions the value on the left by the one on the right. At that point, it appoints it to the articulation on the left.

1. >>> a/=7

2. >>> print(a)

Output: 1.0

e. Duplicate and Assign(*=)

Duplicates the values on either side. At that point, it appoints it to the articulation on the left.

1. >>> a*=8

2. >>> print(a)

Output: 8.00

f. Modules and Assign(%=)

Performs modules on the values on either side. By then, it dispenses it to the enunciation on the left.

1. >>> a%=3

2. >>> print(a)

Output: 2.0

g. Model and Assign(**=)

Performs exponentiation on the values on either side. By then, dispenses it to the enunciation on the left.

1. >>> a**=5

2. >>> print(a)

Output: 32.0

h. Floor-Divide and Assign(//=)

This Performs floor-division on the values on both side. By then, dispenses it to the enunciation on the left.

1. >>> a//=3

2. >>> print(a)

Output: 10.0

This is one of the critical Python Operator.

The Python Logical Operator Command

These are interphases that you can use to join more than one condition. We have three Python logical operators – and, or, and not preposterously go under python operators.

a. also,

In the event that the conditions on both sides of the operator are valid, at that point, the articulation all in all is valid.

1. >>> a=7>7 and 2>-1

2. >>> print(a)

Output: False

b. or on the other hand

The articulation is bogus, just if both the statements around the operator are bogus. Else, it is valid.

1. >>> a=7>7 or 2>-1

2. >>> print(a)

Output: True

'furthermore, restores the principal False value or the last value; 'or' returns the primary True value or the last value.

1. >>> 7 and 0 or 5

Output: 5

c. not

This upsets the Boolean value of an articulation. It changes over True to False, and False to True. As should be obvious underneath, the Boolean value for 0 is False. In this way, not transforms it to True.

1. >>> a=not(0)

2. >>> print(a)

Output: True

Enrollment Python Operator

These operators test whether a value is an individual from an arrangement. The succession might be a list, a string, or a tuple. We have two participation python operators-'in' and 'not in.'

a. in

This checks if a value is an individual from an arrangement. In our model, we see that the string 'fox' doesn't have a place with the lost pets. However, the string 'feline' has a place with it, so it returns True. Likewise, the string 'me' is a substring to the string 'disillusionment.' This way, it returns genuine.

1. >>> pets=['dog','cat','ferret']

2. >>> 'fox' in pets

Output: False

1. >>> 'feline' in pets

Output: True

1. >>> 'me' in 'dissatisfaction'

Output: True

b. not in

Not at all like 'in', 'not in' checks if a value isn't an individual from a grouping.

1. >>> 'pot' not in 'disillusionment'

Output: True

Python Identity Operator

These operators test if the two operands share an identity. We have two identity operators-'is' and 'isn't'.

a. is

If two operands have a similar identity, it returns True. Else, it returns False. Here, 2 isn't equivalent to 20, so it returns False. Additionally, '2' and "2" are the equivalents. The distinction in cites doesn't make them unique. In this way, it returns True.

1. >>> 2 is 20

Output: False

1. >>> '2' will be "2"

Output: True

b. isn't

2 is a number, and '2' is a string. In this way, it restores a True to that.

1. >>> 2 isn't '2'

Output: True

Python Bitwise Operator.

a. Double AND(&)

It performs a little bit at a time AND activity on the two values. Here, double for 2 is 10, and that for 3 is 11. and ing them brings about 10, which is paired for 2. So also, and ing 011(3) and 100(4) brings about 000(0).

1. >>> 2&3

Output: 2

1. >>> 3&4

Output: 0

b. Twofold OR(|)

It performs a tiny bit at a time OR on the two values. Here, OR-ing 10(2) and 11(3) bring about 11(3).

1. >>> 2|3

Output: 3

c. Double XOR(^)

It performs a little bit at a time XOR(exclusive-OR) on the two values. Here, XOR-ing 10(2) and 11(3) bring about 01(1).

1. >>> 2^3

Output: 1

d. Double One's Complement(~)

It restores the one's supplement of a number's paired. It flips the bits. The parallel for 2 is 00000010. Its one's complement is 11111101. This is twofold for - 3. Thus, these outcomes in - 3. Essentially, ~1 results in - 2.

1. >>>~-3

Output: 2

Once more, one's supplement of - 3 is 2.

e. Double Left-Shift(<<)

The value of the left operand moves the number of spots to one side that the correct operand indicates. Here, twofold of 2 is 10. 2<<2 movements it two spots to one side. This outcome is 1000, which is twofold for 8.

1. >>> 2<<2

Output: 8

f. Double Right-Shift(>>)

The value of the left operand movedf the number of spots to the correct that the correct operand determines. Here, double of 3 is 11. 3>>2 movements it two spots to one side. This outcomes in 00, which is twofold for 0. Mostly, 3>>1 movement it one spot to one side. This outcome in 01, which is parallel for 1.

1. >>> 3>>2

2. >>> 3>>1

Output: 1

DIFFERENT FORMS OF PYTHON OPERATORS

Python Bitwise Operators with Syntax and Example

1. Prologue to The Python Bitwise Operators.

Python Bitwise Operators take one to two operands, and works on it/them a little bit at a time, rather than entirety. To take a model, how about we see the 'and' 'and' operators for something very similar.

How about we take two numbers-5 and 7. We'll show you their double counterparts utilizing the function container().

1. >>> bin(5)

'0b101'

1. >>> bin(7)

'0b111'

Presently we should take a stab at applying 'and' 'and' to 5 and 7.

1. >>> 5 and 7

7

1. >>> 5&7

5

You would have anticipated that they should restore something very similar. However they're not the equivalent. One follows up, all in all value, and one follows up on each piece without a moment's delay.

All things considered 'and' sees the value on the left. On the off chance that it has a True Boolean value, it returns whatever value is on the right. Else, it returns False. Along these lines, here, 5 and 7 are equivalent to True and 7. Consequently, it returns 7. Be that as it may, 5&7 is equivalent to 101&111. This outcome in 101, which is paired for 5.

2. Python Bitwise (&) Operator

1numeric has a Boolean value of True, and 0 has that of False. Investigate the accompanying code.

1. >>> True/2

0.5

1. >>> False*2

0

This demonstrates something. Presently, the double (and) takes two values and plays out an AND-ing on each pair of bits. We should take a model.

1. >>> 4 and 8

Paired for 4 is 0100, and that for 8 is 1000. So when we AND the comparing bits, it gives us 0000, which is parallel for 0. Henceforth, the output.

Coming up next are the values when and ing 0 and 1.

Table.1 Python Bitwise Operators – AND Operators

0 and 0 0

0 and 1 0

1 and 0 0

1 and 1 1

As should be obvious, an and ing returns 1 in particular if the two bits are 1.

You can't, notwithstanding, and strings.

1. >>> '$'&'%'

Traceback (latest call last):

Record "<pyshell#30>", line 1, in <module>

'$'&'%'

TypeError: unsupported operand type(s) for and: 'str' and 'str'

Since Boolean values True and False have proportional whole number values of 1 and 0, we can and them.

1. >>> False&True

Bogus

1. >>> True&True

Genuine

How about we attempt a couple of more blends.

1. >>> 1&True

1

1. >>> 1.0&1.0

Traceback (latest call last):

Document "<pyshell#36>", line 1, in <module>

1.0&1.0

TypeError: unsupported operand type(s) for and: 'buoy' and 'buoy'

1. >>> 0b110 and 0b101

4

Here, 110 is double for 6, and 101 for 5. and ing them, we get 100, which is double for 4.

3. Python Bitwise OR (|) Operators

Presently let's talk about Python Bitwise OR (|) Operator

Contrasted with and this one returns 1 regardless of whether one of the two comparing bits from the two operands is 1.

Table.2 Python Bitwise Operators – OR Operators

0|0 0

0|1 1

1|0 1

1|1 1

1. >>> 6|1

7

This is equivalent to the accompanying.

1. >>> 0b110|0b001

7

How about we see some more models.

1. >>> True|False

Genuine

4. Python Bitwise XOR (^) Operator

XOR (eXclusive OR) returns 1 on the off chance that one operand is 0 and another is 1. Else, it returns 0.

Table.1 Python Bitwise Operators – XOR Operators

0^0 0

0^1 1

1^0 1

1^1 0

How about we consider a couple of models.

1. >>> 6^6

Here, this is equivalent to 0b110^0b110. These outcomes in 0b000, which is parallel for 0.

1. >>> 6^0

6

This is identical to 0b110^0b000, which gives us 0b110. This is parallel for 6.

1. >>> 6^3

5

Here, 0b110^0b011 gives us 0b101, which is parallel for 5.

5. Bitwise 1's Complement (~)

This one is somewhat unique in relation to what we've examined up until now. This operator takes a number's parallel and returns its one's supplement. For this, it flips the bits until it arrives at the initial 0 from the right. ~x is equivalent to - x-1.

1. >>> ~2

- 3

1. >>> bin(2)

'0b10'

1. >>> container(- 3)

'- 0b11'

To make it unmistakable, we notice the double values of both. Another model pursues.

1. >>> ~45

- 46

1. >>> bin(45)

'0b101101'

1. >>> receptacle(- 46)

'- 0b101110'

6. Python Bitwise Left-Shift Operator (<<)

At long last, we land at left-move and right-move operators. The left-move operator moves the bits of the number by the predefined number of spots. This implies it adds 0s to the unfilled least-noteworthy places now. How about we start with an irregular model.

1. >>> True<<2

4

Here, True has an equal number value of 1. In the event that we move it by two spots to one side, we get 100. This is twofold for 4.

Presently how about we do it on whole numbers.

1. >>> 2<<1

4

10 moved by one spot to one side gives us 100, which is, once more, 4.

1. >>> 3<<2

12

Presently, 11 moved to one side by two spots gives us 1100, which is twofold for 12.

7. Python Bitwise Right-Shift Operator (>>)

Presently we'll see something very similar for right-move. It moves the bits to one side by the predefined number of spots. This implies those numerous bits are lost at this point.

1. >>> 3>>1

1

3 has a paired value of 11, which moved one spot to the correct returns 1. However, before shutting on this instructional exercise, we'll take one final model.

How about we check what's the decimal value for 11111.

1. >>> int(0b11111)

31

Presently, how about we move it three spots to one side.

1. >>> 31>>3

3

As should be obvious, it gives us 3, whose parallel is 11. Bodes well, isn't that right?

Python Comparison Operators with Syntax and Examples

1. Python Comparison Operators

An examination operator in python, likewise called python social operator, analyzes the values of two operands and returns True or False depending on whether the condition is met. We have six of these, including and constrained to-not exactly, more noteworthy than, not exactly or equivalent to, more prominent than or equivalent to, equivalent to, and not equivalent to. In this way, we should start with the Python Comparison operators.

2. Python Less Than (<) Operator

The principal correlation operator in python we'll see here is the not as much as the operator. Meant by <, it checks if the left value is lesser than that on the right.

1. >>> 3<6

Output: is True

Since 6 is greater than 3, it returns True.

1. >>> 3<3

Output: False

Since 3 is equivalent to 3, and at the very least it, this profits False.

In any case, we should check whether we can apply it to values other than ints.

1. >>> 3<3.0

Output: is false

Here, 3 is an int, and 3.0 is a buoy. However, 3 isn't lesser than 3.0, or the other way around.

1. >>> 3.0<3

Output: False

Presently, how about we give it a shot string.

1. >>> 'Ayushi'<'ayushi'

Output: True

This one outcome is True since when looking at strings, their ASCII values are analyzed. The ASCII value for 'An' is 65. However, that for 'an' is 97. Henceforth, 'An' is lesser than 'a.' Similarly, 'Ayushi' is lesser than 'ayushi'.

If, does it work with Python Booleans?

1. >>> 0.9999999<True

Output: True

Truly, it does. Be that as it may's, captivating that it chips away at compartments like tuples also. We should see a portion of these.

1. >>> (1,2,3)<(1,2,3,4)

Output: True

1. >>> (1,3,2)<(1,2,3)

Output: False

1. >>> (1,2,3)<(1,3,2)

Output: True

1. >>> ()<(0,)

Output: True

Be that as it may, you can't contrast tuples and various types of values.

1. >>> (1,2)<('One','Two')

Traceback (latest call last):

Document "<pyshell#84>", line 1, in <module>

(1,2)<('One','Two')

TypeError: '<' not upheld between occasions of 'int' and 'str'

If you get similar components at similar files, it is conceivable to look at two tuples.

1. >>> (1,'one')<(2,'two')

Output: True

What's more, when we state the same records, we would not joke about this.

1. >>> (1,'one')<('two',2)

Traceback (latest call last):

Record "<pyshell#86>", line 1, in <module>

(1,'one')<('two',2)

TypeError: '<' not bolstered between cases of 'int' and 'str'

1. >>> [0]<[False]

Output: False

1. >>> {1,2,3}<{1,3,2}

Output: False

Here, in light of the fact that the other set adjusts itself to {1,2,3}, the two sets are equivalent. Thusly, it returns False.

1. >>> {1:'one',2:'two'}<{1:'three',2:'four'}

Traceback (latest call last):

Record "<pyshell#91>", line 1, in <module>

{1:'one',2:'two'}<{1:'three',2:'four'}

TypeError: '<' not bolstered between cases of 'dict' and 'dict'

If you face any uncertainty in Python Comparison Operators? If it's not too much trouble, Comment.

3. Python Greater Than (>) Operator

How about we see the Greater than Python Comparison Operator

Since we've seen which develops we can apply these operators to, we will concentrate on the operators now on. The more noteworthy than an operator, meant by >, checks whether the left value is more prominent than the one on the right.

1. >>> 0.5>False

Output: True

1. >>> 3,4,5>3,4,5.0

Output: (3, 4, True, 4, 5.0)

Hello, this made a tuple when all we needed to do was think about it. This is on the grounds that it is accepting 5>3 as a value (True). It put this as a value in the tuple. So how about we attempt to discover our way around this.

1. >>> 3,4,5 > 3,4,5.0

Output: (3, 4, True, 4, 5.0)

So we see that the spaces didn't do it. We should take a stab at something different.

1. >>> 3,4,5>(3,4,5.0)

Traceback (latest call last):

Record "<pyshell#96>", line 1, in <module>

3,4,5>(3,4,5.0)

TypeError: '>' not bolstered between cases of 'int' and 'tuple'

Gee, we think we have to put enclosures around both tuples.

1. >>> (3,4,5)>(3,4,5.0)

Output: False

4. Not exactly or Equal To (<=) Operator

We surmise the following two operators won't be quite a bit of an issue with you. We will quickly figure out how to compose not exactly or equivalent to in Python.

The not exactly or equivalent to the operator, signified by <=, returns True just if the value on the left is either not exactly or equivalent to that on the privilege of the operator.

1. >>> a=2

2. >>> a<=a*2

Output: True

5. Equivalent To or Greater Than – Python (>=) Operator

In like manner, this operator returns True just if the value on the left is more noteworthy than or equivalent to that on the right.

1. >>> from math import pi

2. >>> 3.14>=pi

Output: False

Any uncertainty in Python Comparison Operators? If it's not too much trouble Ask us in the remark.

6. Python Equal To (==) Operator

The last two operators we'll be taking a gander at are equivalent to (==) and not equivalent to (!=).

The equivalent to operator returns True if the values on either side of the operator are equivalent.

1. >>> 3=='3'

Output: False

As we probably are aware, 3 is a whole number, and '3' is a string. Consequently, they're inconsistent. We should take about a couple more models.

1. >>> {1,3,2}=={1,2,3}

Output: True

Like you know, a set revises itself. This is the reason these profits True.

1. >>> 0==False

Output: True

Obviously, False has a whole number value of 0. Consequently, it returns True.

7. Python Not Equal Operator (!=) Operator

At last, we'll talk about not equivalent to the operator. Signified by !=, this does the accurate inverse of the equivalent to the operator. It returns to True if the values on either side of the operator are inconsistent.

1. >>> 3!=3.0

Output: False

1. >>> 3==3.0

Output: True

Note that the operator <> for a similar reason for existing is never again functional.

This is about the Python Comparison Operators.

PYTHON OPERATOR OVERLOADING AND PYTHON MAGIC METHODS

In the programming scene, operator over-burdening is likewise called Operator Ad-hoc Polymorphism. In fact, it is an instance of polymorphism where various operators have various executions dependent on their contentions. This is either characterized by the developer, by the programming language, or both.

Along these lines, how about we start the Python Magic Methods Tutorial.

1. What is Python Operators Overloading?

In Python, an operator lets us play out an activity/method on at least one operand (values). Find out about our article on Python Operators. Be that as it may, for the time being, how about we take a model.

1. >>> 42+1

43

Here, we played out the expansion of two numbers utilizing the expansion operator. You realize that we can apply this operator to Python string too. All things considered, we call it the connection operator. We should examine Python Syntax before continuing.

1. >>> '42'+'1'

'421'

1. >>> 'hello'+' '+'world'

'hi, world.'

And afterward, when we do this to the Python list, we link two lists.

1. >>> [1,2,3]+[4,5,6]

[1, 2, 3, 4, 5, 6] Python does this certainly, however what for when you need to apply this operator to your very own class? Will we? We should check out it.

In this python operator over-burdening instructional exercise, we take a class 'myfloat' to speak to coasting point numbers.

```
1. >>> class myfloat:

2. def __init__(self,whole,fraction):

3. self.whole=whole

4. self.fraction=fraction

5. def shownumber(self):

6. print(f"I am {self.whole}.{self.fraction}")

7. >>> obj1=myfloat(3,7)

8. >>> obj1.shownumber()

I am 3.7

1. >>> obj2=myfloat(3,3)

2. >>> obj2.shownumber()

I am 3.3
```

Presently, we should have a go at including two items.

1. >>> obj1+obj2

Traceback (latest call last):

Document "<pyshell#24>", line 1, in <module> obj1+obj2

TypeError: unsupported operand type(s) for +: 'myfloat' and 'myfloat'

As should be obvious, this raised a TypeError. Be that as it may, don't worry; we can do this, we'll talk about in a later segment.

2. Python Magic Methods

These are extraordinary techniques and are likewise called 'dunders'. These assist us with actualizing functionality that an ordinary strategy can't speak to.

At this point, we have gone over just a single enchantment strategy __init__(). In any case, we can, actually, characterize our own enchantment techniques to actualize operator over-burdening in Python. With this, we can characterize these operators to chip away at our custom classes. A portion of these are-

a. Python Binary Operators

__add__ for +

__sub__ for –

__mul__ for *

__truediv__ for/

__floordiv__ for/

__mod__ for %

__pow__ for **

__and__ for and

__xor__ for ^

__or__ for |
__lshift__ for <<

__rshift__ for >>

b. Python Extended Assignments

__iadd__ for +=

__isub__ for - =

__imul__ for *=

__idiv__ for/=

__ifloordiv__ for/=

__imod__ for %=

__ipow__ for **=

__ilshift__ for <<=

__irshift__ for >>=

__iand__ for &=

__ixor__ for ^=

__ior__ for |=

c. Python Unary Operators

__neg__ for −

__pos__ for +

__abs__ for abs()

__invert__ for ~

__complex__ for complex()

__int__ for int()

__long__ for long()

__float__ for skim()

__oct__ for oct()

__hex__ for hex()

d. Python Comparison Operators

__lt__ for <

__le__ for <=

__eq__ for ==

__ne__ for !=

__ge__ for >=

__gt__ for >

Others incorporate __radd__ for turn around include.

1. >>> class myclass:

2. def __init__(self,age):

3. self.age=age

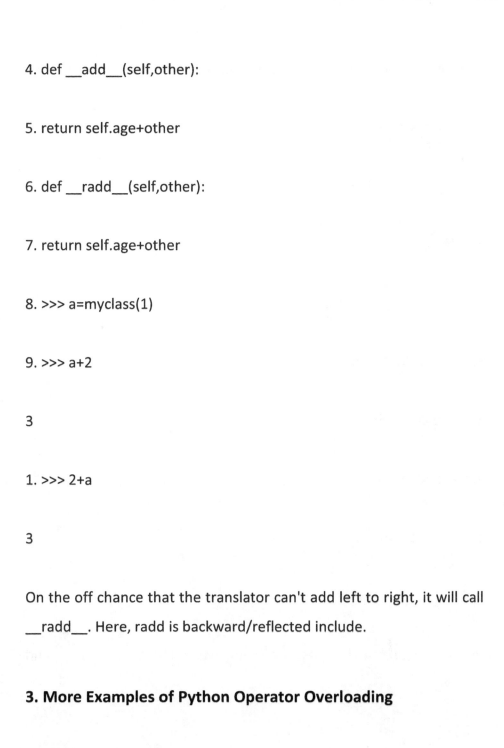

4. def __add__(self,other):

5. return self.age+other

6. def __radd__(self,other):

7. return self.age+other

8. >>> a=myclass(1)

9. >>> a+2

3

1. >>> 2+a

3

On the off chance that the translator can't add left to right, it will call __radd__. Here, radd is backward/reflected include.

3. More Examples of Python Operator Overloading

To truly get something, once is rarely enough. Along these lines, how about we take another case of Operator over-burdening in Python.

```
1. >>> class itspower:

2. def __init__(self,x):

3. self.x=x

4. def __pow__(self,other):

5. return self.x**other.x

6. >>> a=itspower(2)

7. >>> b=itspower(10)

8. >>> a**b

1024
```

In this, we take a class 'itspower' and two techniques __init__ and __pow__.

__pow__ takes two articles and returns the 'x' of first raised to the intensity of the 'x' of the second. At the point when we type a**b, the mediator changes over it certainly to a.__pow__(b).

Presently, we should take another guide to exhibit not many all the more such enchantment techniques.

1. >>> class Person:

2. def __init__(self,name,age):

3. self.name=name

4. self.age=age

5. def __gt__(self,other):

6. if self.age>other.age:

7. return True

8. return False

9. def __abs__(self):

10. return abs(self.age)

11. def __iadd__(self,other):

12. return self.age+other.age

13. >>> Nick=Person('Nick',7)

14. >>> Angela=Person('Angela',5)

15. >>> Nick>Angela

Genuine

1. >>> Kim=Person('Kim',- 8)

2. >>> abs(Kim)

8

1. >>> Tom=Person('Tom',7)

2. >>> Mikayla=Person('Mikayla',3)

3. >>> Tom+=Mikayla

4. >>> Tom

10

To leave this exercise on a drawing in the note, we might simply want to leave this code here:

1. >>> '1'.__add__('1')

'11'

1. >>> 1.__add__(1)

SyntaxError: invalid syntax

1. >>> [1,2,3].__add__([4,5,6])

[1, 2, 3, 4, 5, 6]

Along these lines, this was about Python Operator over-burdening and Python Magic Method Tutorial. Expectation you like it.

The Python Ternary & Operators – 5 Ways To Implement Ternary Operators

1. Python Ternary Operator Example

Ternary operators in Python are short restrictive articulations. These arethe type operators that test a condition and dependent on that, assess a value. This was made accessible since PEP 308 was affirmed and is accessible as far back as variant 2.4. This operator, whenever utilized appropriately, can decrease code size and upgrade clarity.

Do you think about Python Comparison Operator

a. Python if-else code

How about we compose code to analyze two whole numbers.

1. >>> a,b=2,3

2. >>> if a>b:

3. print("a")

4. else:

5. print("b")

b

b. Identical code with Ternary operator

So, if we take a stab at doing likewise with ternary operators:

1. >>> a,b=2,3

2. >>> print("a" if a>b else "b")

b

Voila! Done in one line. Python initially assesses the condition. Assuming genuine, it assesses the primary articulation; else, it assesses the second. There is a sluggish assessment. It additionally assesses the conditions left to right.

2. The syntax for Python Ternary Operator

Presently, how about we get familiar with a little the syntax for Python Ternary Operator.

1. [on_true] if [expression] else [on_false]

In C++, it would appear that this:

1. max=(a>b)?a:b

In any case, this isn't exactly Pythonic, so Guido, Python's BDFL (a status from which he has surrendered forever), dismissed it. Another purpose behind the veto is that we, as of now, have numerous utilizations for the colon(:).

One more case of Python ternary Operators:

1. >>> from arbitrary import irregular

2. >>> a,b=random(),random()

3. >>> res="a" if a>b else "b"

4. >>> res

'b'

1. >>> a,b

(0.009415785735741311, 0.9675879478005226)

3. Approaches to Implement Ternary Operator

Underneath, we are examining various methods for actualizing Python Ternary Operator:

Approaches to Implement Ternary Operator

a. Utilizing Python Tuples

We can utilize tuples to determine what to do if the condition is True/False.

Before proceeding onward, you should find out a little about Python Tuples.

1. >>> a,b=random(),random()

2. >>> (b,a)[a>b]

0.8182650892806171

This is proportional to:

1. >>> (b,a)[True]

Yet, we're befuddled which this is-an or b. We should take a stab at tweaking this.

1. >>> (f"b:{b}",f"a:{a}")[a>b]

'b:0.8182650892806171'

Now we're talking. Taking a gander at the code, you'll figure the main contention in the tuple relates to a Boolean value of False; the second-True. This is a direct result of False=0 and True=1. The condition lives inside the [ ].

Note that this strategy assesses the two components of the tuple, and thus is less productive. This happens if it should initially assemble the tuple before it can search for a list.

1. >>> condition=True

2. >>> 2 if condition else 1/0 #Follows the ordinary if-else rationale tree

2

1. >>> (1/0,2)[condition]

Traceback (latest call last):

Record "<pyshell#48>", line 1, in <module>

(1/0,2)[condition]

ZeroDivisionError: division by zero

b. Utilizing Python Dictionaries

In like manner, we can get this going utilizing lexicons with a similar rationale.

1. >>> a,b=random(),random()

2. >>> {False:f"b:{b}",True:f"a:{a}"}[a>b]

'a:0.37237928632774675'

Since we determine what to do when here, we can trade the places of key-value sets.

1. >>> {True:f"a:{a}",False:f"b:{b}"}[a>b]

'a:0.37237928632774675'

c. Utilizing Lambdas

We can likewise utilize Python Lambda Functions to go about as a ternary operator.

1. >>> (lambda :f"b:{b}",lambda :f"a:{a}")[a>b]()

'b:0.5955717855531699'
4. Settled Python Ternary Operator

We should take a stab at anchoring these operators, will we?

1. >>> a=random()

2. >>> "Under zero" if a<0 else "Somewhere in the range of 0 and 1" if a>=0 and a<=1 else "More noteworthy than one"

'Somewhere in the range of 0 and 1'

View Python Closure

1. >>> A

0.835375743333103878

Here, it is importanat to check for the value of a. On the off chance that it falls shorter than 0, we print "Under zero"; if somewhere in the range of 0 and 1, we print "Somewhere in the range of 0 and 1". Else, we print "More noteworthy than one". Notice how we settled them.

5. Prior to Ternary Operators in Python

Prior to this was a thing with Python, this is the thing that we did (we utilized a common maxim):

1. >>> a,b=2,3

2. >>> a<b and an or b

2

So how does this work? How about we see.

- a is 2 and b is 3

- It checks if a<b

- If genuine, it gives us True and a or b

- This gives us a or b

- It checks a

- If bogus, it gives us False or b

- This gives us b

This strategy, be that as it may, doesn't work for a=0. This is on the grounds that that would be True and 0 or b, which is True and False or b, which is False or b, which is b. Oh no!

Presently why not take a stab at defining an articulation for a>b and have a go at disclosing it to yourself?

It could likewise be advantageous to utilize the or potentially rationale when one of our appearances is equivalent to the condition:

1. >>> def sayhello(): print('Hello')

2. >>> sayhello() if sayhello() else 'Bye'

Hi

Hi

Genuine

1. >>> sayhello() or 'Bye'

Hi

Genuine

PYTHON EXPRESSION

Before we can inform you regarding which operator starts things out, you'd need to be acquainted with articulations. An articulation is a blend of values, factors, operators, and function calls. Strikingly, the Python translator can assess a legitimate articulation. For what reason don't we take a model?

1. >>> 4+3

7

4+3 is an articulation with one operator. We can likewise place in more than one. The priority rules show us the best approach to pursue a request. The division has a higher priority than expansion.

1. >>> 3+3/3

4.0

At the point when we use brackets, in any case, we can adjust the request for execution here.

1. >>> (3+3)/3

2.0

What we finish up here is that utilizing brackets, we can constrain the operators of lower priority to run first. Or then again, we can say that when two operators share an operand, the one with the higher priority gets the opportunity to go first.

1. Python Operator Precedence – PEMDAS

In case you're on this page finding out about Python, you sure have caught wind of BODMAS someplace in your adventure up until now (science, school). In Python, in any case, we run over PEMDAS:

Brackets

Exponentiation

Multiplication

Division

Expansion

Subtraction

A memory helper to recall that will be "Please Excuse My Dear Aunt Susie."

How about we take a model.

1. >>> ((((13+5)*2)- 4)/2)- 13

3.0

How did that occur? We should work it out.

13+5 gives us 18

18*2 gives us 36

36-4 gives us 32

32/2 gives us 16.0 #Note that division gives us skims!

16-13 gives us 3.0

2. Python Operator Precedence – Short-Circuiting

Python consistently assesses the left operand before the right-even in function contentions. For articulations with or potentially tasks, it utilizes shortcircuiting. This implies it assesses the second operand just until it is required. Along these lines, such statements can work dependably:

>>> if(s!=None) and (len(s)<10): pass

To short out is to quit executing the Boolean activity on the off chance that we have just landed at the reality value of the articulation. How about we investigate this:

• X or Y-Evaluates Y just if X is bogus; something else returns X

• X and Y-Evaluates Y just if X is valid; something else, returns X

a. Shortcircuiting with or potentially

See what this gives us:

1. >>> 0 or "Hi" and 1

1

This doesn't give us "Hi", however, 1, in light of the fact that:

0 or "Hi" gives us "Hi"

"Hi" and 1 gives us 1

b. Shortcircuiting with all()/any()

This likewise works with the all() and any() functions.

1. >>> def check(i):

2. return I

3. >>> all(check(i) for I in [1,1,0,0,3])

Bogus

This stops at the main False it gets (the 0 at the third position) and returns False.

1. >>> any(check(i) for I in [0,0,0,1,3])

Genuine

This stops at the primary True it gets (the 1 at the fourth position) and returns True.

c. Shortcircuiting with Conditional Operators

Watch how this spreads out with restrictive operators like > and <.

1. >>> 7>8>check(4)

Bogus

This stops at 7>8 and returns False.

d. Shortcircuiting with Ternary Operators

Presently, consider the accompanying articulation which is a ternary operator:

1. >>> print("One") if print("Two") else print("Three")

Two

Three

What occurs here? Allow's find to out.

Python first checks the condition print("Two"). In assessing this, it prints "Two". Additionally, the Boolean value for this is False:

1. >>> bool(print("Two"))

Two

Bogus

Since it is False, it doesn't assess print("One") and just assesses print("Three").

Subsequently, the last output we get is:

Two

Three

3. Associativity of Operators in Python

In that table above, numerous cells had more than one operator. These offer priority. So at that point, which to assess first? Associativity acts as the hero here. Numerous operators have left-to-right associativity.

a. Cooperative Operators
• Multiplication (*) and Floor Division (//)

For a model, we should consider the operator's multiplication(*) and floor division(//). Watch how the left operand assesses first:

1. >>> 3*5//4

3

1. >>> 3*(5//4)

3

While both give us a similar outcome, they do that in various ways. Watch how:

For the principal model:

3*5 gives us 15

15//4 gives us 3

For the subsequent model:

5//4 gives us 1

3*1 gives us 3

• Exponentiation (**)

Presently, how about we give this a shot exponentiation:

1. >>> (2**3)**2

64

Furthermore, presently without brackets:

1. >>> 2**3**2

512

This is on the grounds that this is proportional to:

2**(3**2)

This gives us 2**9

This gives us 512

b. Non-Associative Operators

Task and examination operators are not cooperative. This means x<y<z is none of the accompanying:

(x<y)<z

x<(y<z)

This articulation is really identical to (and this assesses left-to-right):

x<y and y<z

COMMON PYTHON ERRORS

The 8 Most Common Python Programming Errors

Each engineer on the planet commits errors. Be that as it may, thinking about common slip-ups will spare you time and exertion later. The accompanying list enlightens you regarding the most common errors that designers experience when working with Python:

• Using the off base indentation: Many Python highlights depend on indentation. For instance, when you make another class, everything in that class is indented under the class revelation. The equivalent is valid for choice, circle, & other auxiliary statements. In the event that you find that your code is executing an undertaking when it truly shouldn't be, start assessing the indentation you're utilizing.

• Relying on the task operator rather than the balance operator: When playing out a correlation between two items of value, you simply utilize the equity operator (==), not the task operator (=). The task operator puts an article or value inside a variable and doesn't look at anything.

• Placing function calls in an inappropriate request while making complex statements: Python consistently executes functions from left to right. So the statement MyString.strip().center(21, "*") produces an unexpected outcome in comparison to MyString.center(21, "*").strip(). At the point when you experience a circumstance where the output of a progression of connected functions is unique in relation to what you expected, you have to check function request to guarantee that each function is in the right spot.

• Misplacing punctuation: You can place punctuation in an inappropriate place and make a totally unique outcome. Recollect that you should incorporate a colon toward the finish of each auxiliary statement. Likewise, the situation of enclosures is basic. For example, (1 + 2) * (3 + 4), 1 + ((2 * 3) + 4), and 1 + (2 * (3 + 4)) all produce various outcomes.

• Using the wrong logical operator: Most of the operators don't present designers with issues, yet the logical operators do. Make sure to utilize and to decide when the two operands must be True as well as when both of the operands can be True.

• Creating check by-one errors on circles: Remember that a circle doesn't tally the last number you indicate in a range. Along these lines, if you determine the range [1:11], you really get output for values somewhere in the range of 1 and 10.

• Using an inappropriate capitalization: Python is case touchy, so MyVar is not quite the same as myvar and MYVAR. Continuously check capitalization when you find that you can't get to a value you expected to get to.

• Making a spelling botch: Even prepared designers experience the ill effects of spelling errors now and again. Guaranteeing that you utilize a common way to deal with naming factors, classes, and functions helps. Be that as it may, even a steady naming plan won't generally keep you from composing MyVer when you intended to type MyVar.

In case you're a fledgling level Python developer working with ArcGIS ideally, this will help get you past the halfway point. Underneath, you will discover my list of the 10 most common errors in no specific request.

1. Typos – This ought to presumably abandon in any event, saying, however, typos are the most common and predictable misstep. At the point when you get an error in your code, this ought to presumably be the primary thing you check. Ensure that when you reference a variable someplace in your code that the variable name you're alluding to is spelled precisely as you characterized the variable name before. Here's a model:

```
layerParcel = "Roads"
```

```
… .. #code
```

```
… .. #code
```

```
… .. #code
```

```
on the off chance that lyerParcel == "Roads": #notice that I forgot
about the 'an' in layerParcel
```

2. Python is case delicate – This is presumably the most common non-grammatical error that I stumble into when instructing Python to start level developers. This implies, for instance, that the Python translator will consider them to be as totally various factors.

```
mapsize = "34x44"
```

```
MapSize = "22x32"
```

It's normal to see new software engineers characterize a variable with an alternate blend of packaging (MapSize); however, afterward, endeavor to allude to the variable utilizing an alternate blend of the case (map size), which brings about an error.

3. Indentation – Python utilizes indentation. Python functions have no express start or end, and no wavy supports to stamp where the function code starts and stops. The main delimiter is a colon (:) and the indentation of the code itself. See the model underneath:

```
import arcpy.mapping as mapping

mxd = mapping.MapDocument("CURRENT")

for df in mapping.ListDataFrames(mxd):

for lyr in mapping.ListLayers(mxd, "", df)

in the event that lyr.name == "School Districts":

mapping.RemoveLayer(df, lyr)
```

Code squares are characterized by their indentation. By "code square", I mean functions, if statements, for circles, while circles, etc.

Indenting begins a square, and un-indenting closes it. There are no express props, sections, or catchphrases. This implies whitespace for this situation is noteworthy (typically, it's not in Python yet with regards to indentation for code squares it is), and should be steady. You don't need to incorporate a specific number of spaces, and it simply should be reliable.

You ought to likewise abstain from blending tabs and spaces in the indentation of a given single square. Something else that you find in your proofreader may not be what Python sees when it considers tabs a number of spaces. It's more secure to utilize all tabs or all spaces for each square. The number(s) of spaces is determine you.

4. Make sure to incorporate the colons for compound statements – This is a common fledgling's coding botch: remember to type a: toward the finish of compound statement headers (the primary line of an if, while, for, attempt, with). I would state that a dominant part of my understudies commit this error in any event once and normally ordinarily all through preparing. I think this is halfway in light of the fact that they just don't have a full comprehension of what that colon speaks to, which is that it characterizes the start of a code square.

5. Variable names should start with a letter or underscore – Variables should start with a letter or an underscore. Try not to start a variable name with a number or some other unique character. Likewise, there are sure words that are held and can't be utilized as factor names, including the accompanying:

furthermore, declare, break, class, proceed, def, del, elif, else, with the exception of, executive, at long last, for, from, global, if, import, in, is, lambda, not, or, pass, print, raise, return, attempt, while, yield

6. Instate Your Variables - In Python, you can't utilize a variable name inside an articulation until it has been allotted a value. This is deliberate: it averts common grammatical error botches and maintains a strategic distance from the uncertain inquiry of what a programmed default ought to be (0, None, "", [], ?). Make sure to introduce counters to 0, list gatherers to [], etc.

7. Programmed expansions in windows – If you're coding in something extremely fundamental like Notepad, ensure you unequivocally give your record a .py addition when sparing. Something else, your record will be spared with a .txt expansion, making it hard to run in some starting plans. MS Word and Wordpad likewise include arranging characters as a matter of course that is not lawful Python syntax. You ought to consistently pick All Files when sparing and spare as basic content on Windows, or utilize more software engineer well-disposed editors, for example, IDLE.

Nonetheless, in case you're utilizing IDLE, there is a gotcha with this manager also. You need to make sure to type the .py document expansion when sparing. For reasons unknown, it won't automatically include the .py expansion.

8. More indentation rules – Be certain to begin top-level, un-settled code right to one side. There shouldn't be any space to one side of the mainline of code. Not by any means one space. As I referenced above, Python utilizes indentation to delimit squares of settled code, so blank area to one side of your code implies a settled square. The blank area is commonly disregarded all over the place, with the exception of indentation. I have seen understudies add a solitary space to top-level un-settled code a greater number of times than I can tally. I don't know why that is the situation, but rather it occurs.

9. Use enclosures to call a function – You should include brackets after a function name to call it, regardless of whether it takes contentions or not. An appropriate function call would be affixed () not add. Despite the fact that attach() for this situation needn't bother with any parameters to execute, you do need to incorporate the enclosures to execute the function.

10. Try not to utilize a solitary oblique punctuation line while referencing ways to datasets – A solitary oblique punctuation line in

Python is a getaway character. For instance, Python sees \n as a line feed and \t as a tab. Hence, speaking to a way to a dataset as c:\data\myshapefile.shp will bring about an error. You have a few decisions to determine this. The most effortless approach to deal with this issue is to incorporate a lowercase 'r' before the way as in r"c:\data\myshapefile.shp". You could likewise utilize two oblique punctuation lines "c:\\data\\myshapefile.shp" or a solitary forward slice "c:/information/myshapefile.shp".

TIPS FOR LEARNING PYTHON QUICKLY

Python is one of the most mainstream language out there to the extent programming is concerned. With the advancement of this language beginning in the 1980s, it was granted as the most well-known programming language in 2013. Python is an open-source, object-situated, multi-strung programming language that has arrived at across the board appropriation since its introduction to the world. Effortlessness, one of Python's center ways of thinking, has made the open-source programming tongue very well known among novices.

Python is the most effortless language to learn and develop programs quickly and with less code.

For acing python, you should begin with learning the nuts and bolts of python.

The initial phase in learning any programming language is ensuring that you see how to learn. Learning how to learn is ostensibly the most basic expertise associated with PC programming.

Why is realizing how to adapt so significant? The appropriate response is basic: as language develop, libraries are made, and apparatuses are redesigned.

Make It Stick

Here are a few tips to assist you with making the new ideas you are learning as a novice software engineer truly stick:

Tip #1: Code every possible day

Consistency is critical when you are learning another vernacular. We recommend making a promise to code every day. It may be hard to acknowledge. In any case, muscle memory hugy affects programming. Concentrating on the coding normal will genuinely assist work with increasing that muscle memory. In spite of the way that it may seem, by all accounts, to be overpowering from the start, consider starting little with 25 minutes common and working your way up starting there.

Tip #2: Write It Out

As you progress on your adventure as another software engineer, you may think about whether you ought to be taking notes. Truly, you should! Truth be told, look into proposes that taking notes by hand is generally useful for long haul maintenance. This will be particularly gainful for those progressing in the direction of the objective of turning into a full-time designer, the same number of meetings will include composing code on a whiteboard.

When you start dealing with little tasks and projects, composing by hand can likewise assist you with arranging your code before you move to the PC. You can spare a ton of time on the off chance that you work out which functions and classes you will require, just as how they will connect.

Tip #3: Go Interactive!

Regardless of whether you are learning about essential Python information structures (strings, lists, word references, and so forth.) just because, or you are troubleshooting an application, the intelligent Python shell will be one of your best learning instruments. We use it a great deal on this site as well!

To utilize the intuitive Python shell (likewise some of the time called a "Python REPL"), first ensure Python is installed on your PC. We have a step-by-step instructional exercise to assist you with doing that. To enact the intelligent Python shell, basically, open your terminal and run python or python3 relying upon your installation. You can discover progressively explicit bearings here.

Since you have realize how to start the shell, here are a couple of instances of how you can utilize the shell when you are learning:

Realize what activities can be performed on a component by utilizing dir():

```
>>>

>>> my_string = 'I am a string'

>>> dir(my_string)

['__add__', ..., 'upper', 'zfill'] # Truncated for coherence
```

The components that came back from dir() are the entirety of the strategies (for example, activities) that you can apply to the component. For instance:

```
>>>

>>> my_string.upper()

>>> 'I AM A STRING'
```

Notice that we called the upper() strategy. Would you be able to perceive what it does? It makes the entirety of the letters in the string capitalized! Study these implicit techniques under "Controlling strings" in this guide.

Get familiar with the type of a component:

```
>>>
```

```
>>> type(my_string)
```

```
>>> str
```

Utilize the implicit assistance framework to get full documentation:

```
>>>
```

```
>>> help(str)
```

Import libraries and play with them:

```
>>>
```

```
>>> from datetime import datetime

>>> dir(datetime)

['__add__', ..., 'weekday', 'year'] # Truncated for clarity

>>> datetime.now()

datetime.datetime(2019, 3, 14, 23, 44, 50, 851904)
```

Run shell directions:

```
>>>

>>> import os

>>> os.system('ls')

python_hw1.py python_hw2.py README.txt
```

Tip #4: Take Breaks

Exactly when you are learning, it is basic to step away and ingest the thoughts. The Pomodoro Technique is comprehensively used and can empower: you to work for 25 minutes, appreciate a short respite, and a while later repeat the methodology. Taking breaks is essential to having a feasible assessment session, particularly when you are taking in a lot of new information.

Breaks are especially huge when you are investigating. In case you hit a bug and can't actually comprehend what is turning out gravely, appreciate a relief. Step away from your PC, go for a stroll, or converse with a buddy.

In programming, your code must cling to the rules of a language and basis absolutely, so in any occasion, missing a statement will break everything. Receptive points of view have a significant impact.

Tip #5: Become a Bug Bounty Hunter

Looking at hitting a bug, it is inevitable once you start forming complex ventures that you will run into bugs in your code. It transpires all! Do whatever it takes not to let bugs frustrate you. Or maybe, handle these minutes with fulfillment and view yourself as a bug plenitude tracker.

While investigating, it is basic to have a methodological method to manage the help you find where things are isolating. Encountering your code in the solicitation where it is executed and guaranteeing each part works is a remarkable technique to do this.

At the point when you have an idea of where things might be isolating, implant the going with line of code into your substance import pdb; pdb.set_trace() and run it. This is the Python debugger and this will drop you into natural mode. The debugger can similarly be run from the immediate line with python - m pdb <my_file.py>.

Make It Collaborative

At the point when things start to stick, accelerate your learning through a joint exertion. Here are a couple of systems to help you with profiting by working with other expert.

Tip #6: Acclamatice Yourself With Others Who Are Learning

Regardless of the way that coding may have all the earmarks of being separated from everyone else activity, it truly works best when you coordinate. It is basic when you are figuring out how to code in Python that you surround yourself with other people who are adapting moreover. This will empower you to share the tips and misdirects you learn on the way.

Do whatever it takes not to weight in case you don't know anyone. There are many ways to deal with meet others who are vigorous about learning Python.

Tip #7: Teach

It is said that the perfect way to deal with get something is to train it. This is veritable when you are learning Python. There are various ways to deal with do this: whiteboarding with other Python darlings, creating blog passages explaining as of late learned thoughts, recording chronicles in which you explain something you learned, or simply bantering with yourself at your PC. All of these procedures will solidify your seeing similarly as reveal any gaps in your cognizance.

Tip #8: Pair Program

Pair writing computer programs is a framework that incorporates two planners working at one workstation to complete a task. The two specialists switch between being the "driver" and the "pilot." The "driver" makes the code, while the "direct" deals with the basic reasoning and reviews the code as it is created. Switch once in a while to get the benefit of the different sides.

Pair programming has various preferences: it enables you to have someone review your code, yet what's more, see how someone else might be mulling over an issue. Being displayed to various contemplations and points of view will help you in basic reasoning when you came back to coding without any other person.

Tip #9: Ask "Extraordinary" Questions

People reliably state there is nothing of the sort as a horrible request; nonetheless, with respect to programming, and it is possible to represent a request gravely. Right when you are mentioning help from someone who has by zero settings on the issue you are endeavoring to clarify, its best to present GOOD requests by following this shortened form:

• G: Give the setting on what you are endeavoring to do, clearly portraying the issue.

• O: Outline the things you have quite recently endeavored to fix the issue.

• O: Offer your best supposition regarding what the issue might be. This will help the person who is helping you to understand what you are thinking, yet what's more, understand that you have made some finding isolated.

• D: Demo what's happening. Consolidate the code, a traceback blunder message, and an explanation of the means you executed that achieved the mistake. Thusly, the individual causing doesn't have to endeavor to recreate the issue.

Extraordinary requests can save a huge amount of time. Maintaining a strategic distance from any of these means can result in forward and backward discourses that can cause battle. As a fledgling, you have to guarantee you present incredible requests with the objective that you take a shot at passing on your way of reasoning, subsequently that people who help you with willing be happy to continue helping you.

Make Something

Most, if not all, Python fashioners you address will unveil to you that in order to learn Python, you ought to learn by doing. Doing exercises can simply take you up until this point: you gain capability with the most by building.

Tip #10: Build Something, Anything

For novices, there are various little exercises that will really help you with getting sure with Python, similarly as develop the muscle memory that we discussed previously. At the point when you have a solid handle on basic data structures (strings, records, word references, sets), object-arranged programming, and fertilizing the soil classes, it's an incredible chance to start building!

What you create isn't as critical as how you produce it. The journey of the structure is truly what will show you the most. You can simply increase such an incredible sum from scrutinizing Real Python articles and courses. Most of your taking in will begin from using Python to gather something. The issues you will comprehend will show you a lot.

There are various records out there with contemplations for student Python adventures. Here are a couple of plans to kick you off:

- Number estimating game

- Simple calculator application

- Dice move test framework.

- Bitcoin Price Notification Service

If you believe that its difficult to come up with Python practice dares to work on, watch this video. It spreads out a procedure you can use to create a colossal number of undertaking considerations at whatever point you feel stuck.

Tip #11: Contribute to Open Source

In the open-source model, programming source code is available uninhibitedly, and anyone can cooperate. There are various Python libraries that are open-source assignments and take duties. Moreover, various associations appropriate open-source adventures. This suggests you can work with code formed and conveyed by the masters working in these associations.

Adding to an open-source Python adventure is an inconceivable technique to make incredibly significant learning experiences. Assume you decide to display a bug fix request: you present a "pull request" for your fix to be fixed into the code.

Next, the undertaking chiefs will survey your work, giving remarks, and recommendations. This will empower you to adopt best practices for Python programming, just as work on speaking with different engineers.

PERFORMED PYTHON PROGRAMMING EXERCISES ON FUNCTIONS, STRINGS, LISTS, AND MATHEMATICAL CALCULATIONS

Python String Exercise

This String exercise venture is to help Python designer to learn and work on String controls. As you most likely are aware, stings information structure is generally to hold characters' succession information. To play out any programming undertakings in Python, a great comprehension of string control is essential.

This activity is a piece of Python Exercises with Solutions

What remembered for this String exercise?

• The practice contains 10 inquiries and arrangements accommodated each question.

• Each question incorporates a particular String subject you have to learn. At the point when you complete each question, you get progressively acquainted with String activities in Python.

Exercise Question 1: Given a string of odd length more noteworthy 7, return a string made of the center three scorches of a given String

For instance: –

getMiddleThreeChars("JhonDipPeta") → "Plunge"

getMiddleThreeChars("Jasonay") → "child"

Anticipated Output:

Unique String is JhonDipPeta

Center three burns are Dip.

Unique String is Jasonay

Center three burns are a child

Arrangement

```python
def getMiddleThreeChars(sampleStr):

    middleIndex = int(len(sampleStr)/2)

    print("Original String is", sampleStr)

    middleThree = sampleStr[middleIndex-1:middleIndex+2]

    print("Middle three burns are", middleThree)

getMiddleThreeChars("JhonDipPeta")

getMiddleThreeChars("Jasonay")
```

Python Exercise: Find the Max of three numbers

Python Functions: Exercise-1 with Solution

Compose a Python function to discover the Max of three numbers.

Test Solution:-

Python Code:

```python
def max_of_two( x, y ):

on the off chance that x > y:

return x

return y

def max_of_three( x, y, z ):

return max_of_two( x, max_of_two( y, z )

print(max_of_three(3, 6, - 5))
```

Duplicate

Test Output:

6

String Lists

strings lists file

Exercise 6 (and Solution)

Approach the user for a string and print out whether this string is a palindrome or not. (A palindrome is a string that peruses similar advances and in reverse.)

Dialog

Ideas during the current week:

• List ordering

• Strings are lists

List ordering

In Python (and most programming all in all), you start checking lists from the number 0. The main component in a list is "number 0", the second is "number 1", and so forth.

Thus, when you need to get single components out of a list, you can approach a list for that number component:

```
>>> a = [5, 10, 15, 20, 25]

>>> a[3]

20

>>> a[0]

5
```

There is likewise an advantageous method to get sublists between two files:

```
>>> a = [5, 10, 15, 20, 25, 30, 35, 40]

>>> a[1:4]

[10, 15, 20]

>>> a[6:]

[35, 40]
```

```
>>> a[:- 1]
```

[5, 10, 15, 20, 25, 30, 35]

The main number is the "start list" and the last number is the "end file."

You can likewise remember a third number for the ordering, to check how frequently you should peruse from the list:

```
>>> a = [5, 10, 15, 20, 25, 30, 35, 40]
```

```
>>> a[1:5:2]
```

[10, 20]

```
>>> a[3:0:- 1]
```

[15, 10, 5]

To peruse the entire list, simply utilize the variable name (in the above models, an), or you can likewise utilize [:] toward the finish of the variable name (in the above models, a[:]).

Strings are lists

Since strings are lists, you can do to strings everything that you do to lists. You can emphasize through them:

```
string = "model"

for c in string:

print "one letter: " + c
```

Will give the outcome:

one letter: e

one letter: x

one letter: a

one letter: m

one letter: p

one letter: l

one letter: e

You can take sublists:

>>> string = "model"

>>> s = string[0:5]

>>> print s

example

Presently s has the string "example" in it.

The lesson of the story: a string is a list.

Python Math: Calculate surface volume and zone of a chamber

Python Math: Exercise-5 with Solution

Compose a Python program to compute surface volume and region of a chamber.

Note: A chamber is one of the essential curvilinear geometric shapes, the surface framed by the focuses at a fixed good way from a given straight line, the pivot of the chamber.

Test Solution:-

Python Code:

```
pi=22/7

tallness = float(input('Height of chamber: '))

radian = float(input('Radius of chamber: '))

volume = pi * radian * radian * tallness

sur_area = ((2*pi*radian) * tallness) + ((pi*radian**2)*2)

print("Volume is: ", volume)

print("Surface Area is: ", sur_area)

Duplicate
```

Test Output:

The tallness of chamber: 4

Range of chamber: 6

Volume is: 452.57142857142856

Surface Area is: 377.1428571428571

Python Math: Find the littlest numerous of the main n numbers

Keep going update on November 09 2019 06:56:17 (UTC/GMT +8 hours)

Python Math: Exercise-10 with Solution

Compose a Python program to locate the littlest various of the primary n numbers. Additionally, show the components.

Test Solution:-

Python Code:

```python
def smallest_multiple(n):

    l = n * 2

    factors = [number for number in range(n, 1, - 1) if number * 2 > n]

    print(factors)

    while True:

        for an in factors:

            in the event that l % a != 0:

                l += n

                break

            in the event that (a == factors[-1] and l % a == 0):

                return l

print(smallest_multiple(13))
```

```
print(smallest_multiple(11))
```

Duplicate

Test Output:

[13, 12, 11, 10, 9, 8, 7]

360360

[11, 10, 9, 8, 7, 6]

27720

Python: Sum every one of the things in a list

Python List: Exercise-1 with Solution

Compose a Python program to total every one of the things in a list.

Model - 1 :

Model - 2 :

Model - 3 :

Model - 4 :

Test Solution:-

Python Code:

```python
def sum_list(items):

    sum_numbers = 0

    for x in things:

        sum_numbers += x

    return sum_numbers

print(sum_list([1,2,- 8]))
```

Python List: Exercise-5 with Solution

Compose a Python program to tally the number of strings where the string length is at least 2, and the first and last character are the same from a given list of strings.

Test Solution:-

Python Code:

```
def match_words(words):

ctr = 0

for word in words:

on the off chance that len(word) > 1 and word[0] == word[-1]:

ctr += 1

return ctr

print(match_words(['abc', 'xyz', 'aba', '1221']))
```

Python Exercise: Find the Max of three numbers

Keep going update on November 09 2019 06:56:16 (UTC/GMT +8 hours)

Python Functions: Exercise-1 with Solution

Compose a Python function to discover the Max of three numbers.

Test Solution:-

Python Code:

```
def max_of_two( x, y ):

on the off chance that x > y:

return x

return y

def max_of_three( x, y, z ):
```

```
return max_of_two( x, max_of_two( y, z )
```

```
print(max_of_three(3, 6, - 5))
```

Python Exercise: Calculate the number of upper/lower case letters in a string

Keep going update on November 09 2019 06:56:17 (UTC/GMT +8 hours)

Python Functions: Exercise-7 with Solution

Compose a Python function that acknowledges a string and figure the number of capitalized letters and lower case letters.

Test Solution:-

Python Code:

```
def string_test(s):
```

```
d={"UPPER_CASE":0, "LOWER_CASE":0}
```

```
for c in s:
```

```python
in the event that c.isupper():

    d["UPPER_CASE"]+=1

elif c.islower():

    d["LOWER_CASE"]+=1

else:

    pass

print ("Original String:, "s)

print ("No. of Upper case characters : ", d["UPPER_CASE"])

print ("No. of Lower case Characters : ", d["LOWER_CASE"])

string_test('The speedy Brown Fox')
```

Duplicate

Test Output:

Unique String: The speedy Brow Fox

No. of Upper case characters : 3

No. of Lower case Characters: 13

TYPES OF LEARNING MACHINE

Machine learning is the field of concentrate that offers PCs the capacity to learn without being specifically customized to do as such.

It's a sub-region of man-made brainpower that licenses PCs to rise into a self-learning mode. Along these lines, when looked to new informational indexes, these PC programs are empowered to learn, develop, and create without anyone else.

Machine Learning Types

Despite the fact that the idea of machine learning is utilized from quite a while prior, the capacity to independently direct complex numerical contemplations to huge informational indexes was accomplished in this field a few years back.

Additionally, there are various types of machine learning, alongside explicit calculations that appropriately work with a particular type of machine learning.

Extensively, there are 3 types of Machine Learning Algorithms.

1. Managed Learning

How it functions: This calculation comprises of an objective/result variable (or ward variable), which is to be anticipated from a given arrangement of indicators (autonomous factors). Utilizing this arrangement of factors, we create a function that guides contributions to wanted outputs. The preparation procedure proceeds until the model accomplishes an ideal degree of exactness on the preparation information.

2. Unaided Learning

How it functions: In this calculation, we don't have any objective or result variable to foresee/gauge. It is utilized for the bunching populace in various gatherings, which is broadly utilized for portioning clients in various gatherings for explicit mediation — instances of Unsupervised Learning: Apriori calculation, K-implies.

3. Support Learning:

How it functions: Using this calculation, the machine is prepared to settle on explicit choices. It works along these lines: the machine is presented to a situation where it trains itself, ceaselessly utilizing experimentation. This machine gains from past understanding and attempts to catch the ideal information to settle on exact business choices. Case of Reinforcement Learning: Markov Decision Process

List of Common Machine Learning Algorithms

Here is the list of commonly utilized machine learning calculations. These calculations can be applied to practically any information issue:

1. Linear Regression

2. Logistic Regression

3. Decision Tree

4. SVM

5. Naive Bayes

6. kNN

7. K-Means

8. Random Forest

9. Dimensionality Reduction Algorithms

10. Gradient Boosting calculations and this is divided into :

A. GBM

B. XGBoost

C. LightGBM

D. CatBoost

1. Linear Regression

It is utilized to gauge genuine values (cost of houses, number of calls, all-out deals, and so on.) in view of the constant variable(s). Here, we build up connections among autonomous and subordinate factors by fitting the best line. This best fit line is known as relapse line and spoke to by a straight condition Y= a *X + b.

The ideal approach to comprehend straight relapse is to remember this experience of adolescence. Allow us to state, and you ask a youngster in fifth grade to orchestrate individuals in his class by expanding request of weight, without asking them their loads! What do you figure the kid will do? He/she would almost certainly look (outwardly break down) at the tallness and work of individuals and organize them utilizing a blend of these obvious parameters. This is a straight relapse, in actuality! The kid has really made sense of that tallness and would be corresponded to the weight by a relationship, which resembles the condition above.

In this condition:

• Y – Dependent Variable

• a – Slope

• X – Independent variable

• b – Intercept

These coefficients an and b are inferred dependent on limiting the whole of squared distinction of separation between information focuses and relapse line.

Straight Regression is for the most part of two types: Simple Linear Regression and Multiple Linear Regression. Straightforward Linear Regression is portrayed by one autonomous variable. What's more, Multiple Linear Regression (as the name recommends) is portrayed by different (multiple) free factors. While finding the best fit line, you can fit a polynomial or curvilinear relapse. Also, these are known as polynomial or curvilinear relapse.

2. Logistic Regression

Try not to get befuddled by its name! It is a classification, not a relapse calculation. It is utilized to appraise discrete values (Binary values like 0/1, yes/no, genuine/bogus) dependent on the given arrangement of the free variable(s). In straightforward words, it predicts the likelihood of the event of an occasion by fitting information to a logic function. Consequently, it is otherwise called logit relapse. Since it predicts the likelihood, its output values lie somewhere in the range of 0 and 1 (true to form).

Once more, let us attempt to comprehend this through a basic model.

Suppose your companion gives you a riddle to unravel. There are just 2 result situations – it is possible that you comprehend it or you don't.

Presently envision that you are being given the wide scope of riddles/tests, trying to comprehend which subjects you are great at. The result of this examination would be something like this – on the off chance that you are given trigonometry based tenth-grade issue, you are 70% prone to settle it. Then again, on the off chance that it is grade fifth history question, the likelihood of finding a solution is just 30%. This is the thing that Logistic Regression gives you.

Moreover.

There are various steps that could be attempted so as to improve the model:

• including communication terms

• removing highlights

• Regularization methods

• using a non-straight model

3. Decision Tree

This is one of my preferred calculations, and I use it oftentimes. It is a type of regulated learning calculation that is, for the most part, utilized for classification issues. Shockingly, it works for both absolute and constant ward factors. In this calculation, we split the populace into at least two homogeneous sets. This is done dependent on most critical traits/autonomous factors to make as unmistakable gatherings as would be prudent.

The ideal approach to see how choice tree functions, is to play Jezzball – a classic game from Microsoft (picture underneath). Basically, you have a stay with moving dividers, and you have to make dividers to such an extent that most extreme region gets tidied up without the balls.

In this way, every time you split the live with a divider, you are attempting to make 2 distinct populaces within a similar room. Choice trees work in fundamentally the same as design by separating a populace in as various gatherings as could be expected under the circumstances.

4. SVM (Support Vector Machine)

It is a classification strategy. In this calculation, we plot every datum thing as a point in n-dimensional space (where n is the number of highlights you have) with the value of each component being the value of a specific organization.

For instance, in the event that we just had two highlights like Height and Hair length of an individual, we'd initially plot these two factors in two-dimensional space where each point has two coordinates (these co-ordinates are known as Support Vectors)

Presently, we will discover some line that parts the information between the two diversely classified gatherings of information. This will be the line with the end goal that the good ways from the nearest point in every one of the two gatherings will be most remote away.

Think about this calculation as playing JezzBall in n-dimensional space. The changes in the game are:

• You can draw lines/planes at any edges (as opposed to simply even or vertical as in the classic game)

• The achievable goal of the game is to isolate bundles of various hues in various rooms.

• And the balls are not moving.

5. Guileless Bayes

It is a classification strategy dependent on Bayes' hypothesis with suspicion of freedom between indicators. In straightforward terms, a Naive Bayes classifier accepts that the nearness of a specific element in a class is random to the nearness of some other component. For instance, an organic product might be viewed as an apple on the off chance that it is red, round, and around 3 crawls in the distance across. Regardless of whether these highlights rely upon one another or upon the presence of different highlights, a credulous Bayes classifier would consider these properties to autonomously add to the likelihood that this organic product is an apple.

Credulous Bayesian model is anything but difficult to fabricate and especially helpful for huge informational indexes. Alongside straightforwardness, Naive Bayes is known to beat even profoundly modern classification strategies.

Here,

• P(c|x) is the back likelihood of class (target) given indicator (property).

• P(c) is the earlier likelihood of class.

• P(x|c) is the probability, which is the likelihood of indicator given class.

• P(x) is the earlier likelihood of indicator.

Model: Let's comprehend it utilizing a model. Beneath I have an informational preparation collection of climate and relating objective variable 'Play'. Presently, we have to classify whether players will play or not founded on climate conditions. We should pursue the underneath steps to perform it.

Step 1: Convert the informational index to recurrence table

Step 2: Create a Likelihood table by finding the probabilities like Overcast likelihood = 0.29, and the likelihood of playing is 0.64.

Step 3: Now, utilize the Naive Bayesian condition to compute the back likelihood for each class. The class with the most noteworthy back likelihood is the result of expectation.

Issue: Players will pay if the climate is bright, is this statement is right?

We can explain it is utilizing the above-examined technique, so P(Yes | Sunny) = P(Sunny | Yes) * P(Yes)/P (Sunny)

Here we have P (Sunny |Yes) = 3/9 = 0.33, P(Sunny) = 5/14 = 0.36, P(Yes)= 9/14 = 0.64

Presently, P (Yes | Sunny) = 0.33 * 0.64/0.36 = 0.60, which has higher likelihood.

Innocent Bayes utilizes a comparative technique to foresee the likelihood of various classes dependent on different properties. This calculation is, for the most part, utilized in content classification and with issues having various classes.

6. kNN (k-Nearest Neighbors)

It very well may be utilized for both classification and relapse issues. Be that as it may, it is all the more broadly utilized in classification issues in the business. K closest neighbors is a straightforward calculation that stores every single accessible case and classifies new cases by a greater part vote of its k neighbors. The case being doled out to the class is generally common among its K closest neighbors estimated by a separation function.

These separation functions can be Euclidean, Manhattan, Minkowski, and Hamming separation. Initial three functions are utilized for ceaseless function and the fourth one (Hamming) for all-out factors. In the event that K = 1, at that point, the case is essentially allowed to the class of its closest neighbor. Now and again, picking K ends up being a test while performing kNN demonstrating.

KNN can without much of a stretch be mapped to our genuine lives. In the event that you need to find out about an individual, of whom you have no data, you may get a kick out of the chance to get some answers concerning his dear companions and the circles he moves in and access his/her data!

Interesting points before choosing kNN:

• KNN is computationally costly

• Variables ought to be standardized; else, higher range factors can inclination it.

• Works on pre-handling stage more before going for kNN like an anomaly, commotion evacuation

7. K-Means

It is a type of solo calculation which takes care of the grouping issue. Its technique pursues a straightforward and simple approach to classify a given informational index through a specific number of groups (expect k bunches). The information focuses on a bunch are homogeneous and heterogeneous to peer gatherings.

Recollect making sense of shapes from ink blotches? K implies it is, to some degree, comparative this action. You take a gander at the shape and spread to unravel what number of various bunches/populace are available!

How K-implies structures bunch:

1. K-implies pick k number of focuses for each group known as centroids.

2. Each information point frames a group with the nearest centroids, for example, k bunches.

3. Finds the centroid of each bunch dependent on existing group individuals. Here we have new centroids.

4. As we have new centroids, rehash steps 2 and 3. Locate the nearest separation for every datum point from new centroids and get related to new k-groups. Rehash this procedure until the union happens. For example, centroids don't change.

Step by step instructions to decide the value of K:

In K-implies, we have bunches, and each group has its very own centroid. The aggregate of the square of contrast among centroid and the information focuses inside a bunch comprises inside the whole of square value for that group. Likewise, when the aggregate of square values for every one of the bunches is included, it gets the aggregate inside the entirety of square value for the group arrangement.

We realize that as the number of the group expands, this value continues diminishing, however, on the off chance that you plot the outcome, you may see that the total of squared separation diminishes pointedly up to some value of k, and afterward substantially more gradually after that. Here, we can locate the ideal number of the bunch.

8. Irregular Forest

Irregular Forest is a trademarked term for a group of choice trees. In Random Forest, we have an assortment of choice trees (so-known as "Woods"). To classify another article dependent on traits, each tree gives a classification, and we state the tree "votes" for that class. The woodland picks the classification having the most votes (over every one of the trees in the timberland).

Each tree is planted and developed as pursues:

1. If the number of cases in the preparation set is N, at that point test of N cases is taken indiscriminately yet with substitution. This example will be the preparation set for developing the tree.

2. If there are M input factors, a number m<<M is determined to such an extent that at every hub, m factors are chosen aimlessly out of the M, and the best split on this m is utilized to part the hub. The value of m is held steady during the timberland developing.

3. Each tree is developed to the biggest degree conceivable. There is no pruning.

9. Dimensionality Reduction Algorithms

In the last 4-5 years, there has been an exponential increment in information catching at each potential stage. Corporates/Government Agencies/Research associations are accompanying new sources as well as they are catching information in extraordinary detail.

For instance: E-trade organizations are catching more insights concerning clients like their socioeconomics, web creeping history, what they like or aversion, buy history, input, and numerous others to give them customized consideration more than your closest basic food item businessperson.

As an information researcher, the information we are offered likewise comprises numerous highlights, and this sounds useful for building a great strong model; however, there is a test. How'd you distinguish exceptionally critical variable(s) out 1000 or 2000? In such cases, dimensionality decrease calculation causes us alongside different calculations like Decision Tree, Random Forest, PCA, Factor Analysis, Identify dependent on relationship lattice, missing value proportion, and others.

10. Slope Boosting Algorithms

10.1. GBM

GBM is a boosting calculation utilized when we manage a lot of information to make a forecast with high expectation control. Boosting is really a group of learning calculations which consolidates the expectation of a few base estimators so as to improve vigor over a solitary estimator. It consolidates various feeble or normal indicators to a form of solid indicator. These boosting calculations consistently function admirably in information science rivalries like Kaggle, AV Hackathon, CrowdAnalytix.

GradientBoostingClassifier and Random Forest are two distinctive boosting tree classifier, and frequently individuals get some information about the contrast between these two calculations.

10.2. XGBoost

Another classic slope is boosting calculation that is known to be the definitive decision among winning and losing in some Kaggle rivalries.

The XGBoost has an enormously high prescient power, which settles on it the best decision for exactness in occasions as it has both direct model and the tree learning calculation, making the calculation practically 10x quicker than existing inclination promoter methods.

The help incorporates different target functions, including relapse, classification, and positioning.

A fascinating aspect concerning the XGBoost is that it is additionally called a regularized boosting method. This diminishes overfit demonstrating and has an enormous help for a scope of language, for example, Scala, Java, R, Python, Julia, and C++.

Supports appropriated and broad preparing on numerous machines that envelop GCE, AWS, Azure, and Yarn bunches. XGBoost can likewise be coordinated with Spark, Flink, and other cloud dataflow frameworks with an inherent cross approval at every emphasis of the boosting procedure.

10.3. LightGBM

LightGBM is an inclination boosting system that utilizations tree-based learning calculations. It is intended to be dispersed and effective with the accompanying focal points:

• Faster preparing speed and higher proficiency

• Lower memory use

• Better precision

• Parallel and GPU learning upheld.

• Capable of taking care of huge scale information

The system is a quick and elite inclination boosting one dependent on choice tree calculations utilized for positioning, classification, and numerous other machine learning errands. It was created under the Distributed Machine Learning Toolkit Project of Microsoft.

Since the LightGBM depends on choice tree calculations, it parts the tree leaf astute with the best fit while other boosting calculations split the tree profundity savvy or level shrewd instead of leaf-wise. So when developing on a similar leaf in Light GBM, the leaf-wise calculation can decrease more misfortune than the level-wise calculation and subsequently brings about much better exactness which can once in a while be accomplished by any of the current boosting calculations.

What is the sort of issues which can be understood utilizing machine learning?

Machine Learning issues can be isolated into three expansive classes:

• **Supervised Machine Learning:** When you have past information with results (marks in machine learning phrasing), and you need to foresee the results for the future – you would utilize Supervised Machine Learning calculations. Regulated Machine Learning issues can again be separated into 2 sorts of issues:

- ○ Classification Problems: When you need to classify results in various classes. For instance – regardless of whether the floor needs cleaning/wiping is a classification issue. The result can be categorized as one of the classes – Yes or No. Essentially, regardless of whether a client would default on their advance or not is a classification issue which is of high enthusiasm to any Bank

- ○ Regression Problem: When you are keen on noting how a lot – these issues would fall under the Regression umbrella. For instance, – how much cleaning should be done is a Regression issue. Or on the other hand, what is the normal measure of default from a client is a Regression issue.

• **Unsupervised Machine Learning:** Sometimes, when you would prefer not to anticipate an Outcome precisely. You simply need to play out a division or grouping. For instance, – a bank would need to have a division of its clients to comprehend their conduct. This is an Unsupervised Machine Learning issue as we are not foreseeing any results here.

• **Reinforcement Learning:** Reinforcement Learning is said to be the desire for genuine man-made consciousness. What's more, it is appropriately said so in light of the fact that the potential that Reinforcement Learning has is monstrous. It is a somewhat complex point when contrasted with conventional machine learning yet a similarly vital one for what's to come. This article is as great a prologue to fortification learning as any you will discover

What are the Different calculations utilized in Machine Learning?

• Supervised Learning

  o   Linear Regression

  o   Logistic Regression

- k-closest neighbors

- Decision Trees

- Random Forest

- Gradient Boosting Machines

- XGBoost

- Support Vector Machines (SVM)

- Neural Networks

- Unsupervised Learning

  - k implies bunching

  - Hierarchical bunching

  - Neural Network

- Reinforcement Learning

For an elevated level comprehension of these calculations, you can watch this video:

For find out about these famous calculations alongside their codes – you can see this article:

• Commonly utilized Machine Learning Algorithms (with Python and R Codes)

What amount of information is required to prepare a machine learning model?

There is no basic response to this inquiry. It relies upon the issue you are attempting to unravel, the expense of gathering gradual information, and the advantages originating from steady information. Here are a few rules:

• In general – you would need to gather; however, much information as could reasonably be expected. On the off chance that the expense of gathering the information isn't extremely high – this winds up working fine.

• If the expense of catching the information is high, at that point, you would need to do a money-saving advantage investigation dependent on the normal advantages originating from machine learning models.

• The information being caught should be illustrative of the conduct/condition you anticipate that the model should chip away at

What sort of information is required to prepare a machine learning model?

Everything which you see, hear, and do is information. All you need is to catch that in the correct way.

Information is inescapable nowadays. From signs on sites and cell phones to wellbeing gadgets – we are in a steady procedure of making information. Actually, 90% of the information in this Universe has been made over the most recent year and a half.

Information can comprehensively be classified into two types:

1. Structured Data: Structured information typically alludes to information put away in an unthinkable configuration in databases in associations. This incorporates information about

clients, connections with them and a few different qualities, which move through the IT framework of Enterprises

2. Unstructured Data: Unstructured Data incorporates every one of the information which gets caught, yet isn't put away as tables in ventures. For instance − letters of correspondence from clients or tweets and pictures from clients. It additionally incorporates pictures and voice records.

Machine Learning models can deal with both Structured just as Unstructured Data if you have to change over unstructured information to organized information first.

What are the steps associated with building machine learning models?

Any machine learning model advancement can comprehensively be partitioned into six steps:

- Problem definition includes changing over a Business Problem to a machine learning issue

- Hypothesis age is the way toward making a potential business theory and potential highlights for the model.

- Data Collection expects you to gather the information for testing your speculation and building the model.

- Data Exploration and cleaning cause you to expel anomalies, missing values, and afterward change the information into the necessary organization.

- Modeling is the place you really fabricate the machine learning models.

- Once fabricated, you will convey the models.

What are probably the most recent accomplishments and improvements in machine learning?
What are the absolute most recent accomplishments and improvements in machine learning?

Probably the most recent accomplishments of machine learning include:

- Winning DOTA2 against the expert players (OpenAI's improvement)

- Beating Lee Sidol at the customary round of GO (Google DeepMind's calculation)

- Google setting aside to 40% of power in its server farms by utilizing Machine Learning

- Writing whole papers and verse, and making films without any preparation utilizing Natural Language Processing (NLP) procedures (Multiple achievements, the most recent being OpenAI's GPT-2)

- Creating and producing pictures and recordings without any preparation (this is both extraordinarily inventive and worryingly precise)

- Building mechanized machine learning models. This is changing the field by growing the hover of individuals who can work with machine learning to incorporate non-specialized people too.

- Building machine learning models in the program itself! (A Google creation – TensorFlow.js)

We really composed a thorough article on the significant AI and machine learning achievements in the previous year, which everybody ought to experience:

• A Technical Overview of AI and ML (NLP, Computer Vision, Reinforcement Learning) in 2018 and Trends for 2019

How great are the machines as of now?

At the present degree of technological progressions, machines are just great at doing explicit undertakings. A machine that has been "instructed" cleaning can just do cleaning (for the present). Indeed, if there is a surface of new material or structure which the machine has not been prepared on – the machine won't have the option to take a shot at it in a similar way.

This is generally not the situation with people. In this way, if an individual is liable for cleaning and wiping, he/she can likewise be security protect. He/she can likewise help in arranging coordinations.

This period of computerized reasoning is typically alluded to as "Fake Narrow Intelligence".

What is a portion of the Challenges in the adOption of Machine Learning?

While machine learning has gained gigantic ground over the most recent couple of years, there are some huge provokes that still should be tackled. It is a territory of dynamic research, and I anticipate that a great deal of exertion should take care of these issues in the coming time.

- Huge information required: It takes a gigantic measure of information to prepare a model today. For instance – if you need to classify Cats versus Pooches dependent on pictures (and you don't utilize a current model) – you would require the model to be prepared on a large number of pictures. Contrast that with a human – we typically clarify the distinction between Cat and Dog to a youngster by utilizing 2 or 3 photographs

- The high figure required: As of now, machine learning and profound learning models require colossal calculations to accomplish straightforward undertakings (basic as indicated by people). This is the reason the utilization of uncommon equipment, including GPUs and TPUs, is required. The expense of calculations needs to descend for machine learning to have a next-level effect

- Interpretation of models is troublesome on occasion: Some displaying strategies can give us high precision yet are hard to clarify. This can leave the entrepreneurs baffled. Envision being a bank, yet you can't explain why you declined an advance for a client!

- New and better calculations required: Researchers are reliably paying special mind to be new and better calculations to address a portion of the issues referenced previously.

- More Data Scientists required: Further since the area has developed so quickly – there aren't numerous individuals with the ranges of abilities required to take care of the tremendous assortment of issues. This is required to remain so for the following barely any years. In this way, on the off chance that you are pondering structure a vocation in machine learning – you are in great stead!

Is Machine Learning a total black box?

You heard me there!

No – it isn't. There are techniques or calculations inside machine learning which can be translated well. These techniques can enable us to comprehend what are the noteworthy connections and why has the machine taken a specific choice.

Then again, there are sure calculations that are hard to translate. With these techniques, regardless of whether we accomplish a high precision, we may battle with clarifications.

Interestingly, contingent upon the application or the issue we are attempting to unravel – we can pick the correct technique. This is additionally an extremely dynamic field of innovative work.

How might I manufacture a profession in Machine Learning?

Presently you are posing the ideal inquiries! Given the deficiency of ability in this area, it unquestionably bodes well to take a gander at building a vocation in information science and machine learning. Before you choose, you should remember the accompanying things:

• You would be OK with coding so as to fabricate a profession as an information researcher. Of course, there are GUI devices accessible –

yet information researchers need to code their very own calculations to be up to speed with the most recent improvements in the area.

• You needn't bother with a foundation or a Ph.D. in science. You can generally get the things you need. On the off chance that you are from this foundation – it helps, yet it isn't required.

• For those changing from some other area or field – plan for in any event year and a half of progress. I you get a break previously – think about this as a little something extra.

Aptitudes expected to construct a vocation in Machine Learning.

Organized reasoning, correspondence, and critical thinking

- This is likely the most significant aptitude required in an information researcher. You have to take business issues and afterward convert them to machine learning issues. This requires putting a structure around the issue and afterward illuminating it. Look at this course to fabricate and sharpen your organized reasoning abilities.

• Mathematics and Statistics

- You need science and measurements to see how the calculations work and what are their restrictions

• Business Understanding

- At the day's end, you will take care of business issues utilizing machine learning. In this way, you would need to have a decent comprehension of the present procedures, impediments, and choices.

• Software Skills

- Data Scientists need to construct calculations, yet they additionally need to code them and coordinate them into the items flawlessly. That is the place programming aptitudes become possibly the most important factor.

CONCLUSION

Programming isn't just about getting a PC to get things done. It is tied in with composing code that is helpful to people. Great programming is saddling complexity by composing code that rhymes with our instincts. Great code will be code that we can use with a negligible amount of setting and right now be gainful.

Python genuinely has a solitary heritage, and it is essential that Python has made quality a progressively focal concentration in the improvement world. It was practically inescapable. A language that requires its users to arrange code for intelligibility can't resist the urge to make individuals bring up issues about great programming practice when all is said in done.

Most Python software engineers today compose unadulterated Python code while never knowing or care about outside libraries. Typically, a little bunch of designers incorporates outside libraries for the dominant part to use in their Python code. While combination still issues, Python is, to a great extent, about quality and efficiency to the vast majority today.

With numerous customary programming devices, you can without much of a stretch lose the timberland for the trees: the demonstration of programming turns out to be intricate to such an extent that this present reality objective of the program is darkened. Customary language occupy important consideration regarding syntactic issues and the advancement of accounting code. Clearly, complexity isn't an end in itself; it must be unmistakably justified. However, a portion of our present devices is mind-boggling to the point that the language itself makes the undertaking harder and protracts the improvement procedure.

Python's advancement cycle is dramatically shorter than that of conventional apparatuses. In Python, there are no accumulate or connection steps - Python programs essentially import modules at runtime and utilize the items they contain. Along these lines, Python programs pursue promptly changes are made. Also, in situations where dynamic module reloading can be utilized, it's even conceivable to change and reload portions of a running system ceaselessly by any stretch of the imagination.